Praise for *Leading Culture Change in Global Organizations*

"A milestone in the culture studies arena."

—Edgar H. Schein, professor emeritus, Massachusetts Institute of Technology

"A page-turner for senior executives that embrace change."

—Cees 't Hart, CEO, FrieslandCampina

"Denison and his colleagues provide the definitive guide for guiding cultural change during these weird and often vexing times. *Leading Culture Change in Global Organizations* grabs you with compelling cases, helps you with fact-based and useful advice, and is the rare business book that is a joy to read."

—Robert I. Sutton, professor, Stanford University; author of *The New York Times* bestseller *Good Boss, Bad Boss*

"I believe 'what gets measured gets done.' The tools and metrics provided by Denison help organizations track their progress and performance in the all-important area of culture. All organizations have a culture, but sadly, many have a culture that doesn't lead to consistent high performance. *Leading Culture Change in Global Organizations* will provide you with a roadmap for creating and maintaining a culture that will provide you with a true competitive advantage. I recommend this book, and the Denison Team, as valuable resources to help you lead more effectively and create a stronger, more results-oriented culture within your organization."

—David A. Brandon, athletic director, University of Michigan; chairman, Domino's Pizza

"Through the real-world examples in *Leading Culture Change in Global Organizations*, the authors bring to life the criticality of culture in global organizations, while providing leaders with an important tool for measuring and transforming it."

—Nancy Dearman, CEO, Kotter International

"The Denison Culture Survey was a pivotal marker in the journey to get our organization focusing more on customers and thinking clearly about our strategy. There's immense power in reflecting on the collective wisdom of the entire team."

—Mike Pulick, president, international, W.W. Grainger, Inc.

"The Marriott culture is integral to our ability to endure and adapt, and to preserve and innovate. This always requires our leaders to rely on the collective wisdom they have developed over the years, and to apply that to the future. The Denison model and method, described so well in this book, helps our leaders to understand the challenges that they face, and helps them to hone in on the key issues and actions that reinforce our culture and help prepare our organization for the future."

—Tim Tobin, vice president, global learning and development, Marriott

"Mastering the levers needed to shape the culture of a global organization is a key task of successful leaders. In line with IMD's vision to support developing global leaders, I highly recommend this valuable book to senior business executives."

—Peter Wuffli, chairman, IMD Foundation Board; former CEO, United Bank of Switzerland

"The beauty of the Denison Culture Model is its simplicity. By remembering that 'more color is better,' you're able to quickly identify your strengths, as well as the areas for improvement to drive action. Most importantly, the model enables dialogue amongst key stakeholders to drive change with a focus on results."

—Robert J. Stuart, senior vice president, global sales and marketing, The Hertz Corporation

"Creating one common culture adjusted to the business portfolio and goals is essential for every company. This book provides many valuable insights to create one overall culture as a competitive advantage."

—Feike Sijbesma, CEO, Royal DSM

"There is hope after all. There is a clear path to growing a strong culture that delivers for customers, staff, shareholders, and the organization. This book is a must-read for any leader that grapples with the scale, pace, and complexity of business today. Keep this book beside you!"

—Phil Morley, chief executive, Hull and East Yorkshire Hospitals, NHS, UK

"In the past, Denison and his colleagues have been pioneers in showing us how culture influences business performance. In this new book, they introduce a new perspective based on rituals, habits, and routines that shows us how to access the tacit organizational knowledge that is the foundation of an organization's culture. If you need to know how to articulate and change the culture of an organization, this book can give you the answer."

—Ikujiro Nonaka, Hitotsubashi University, Tokyo, Japan

The Jossey-Bass
Business & Management Series

LEADING CULTURE CHANGE IN GLOBAL ORGANIZATIONS

Aligning Culture and Strategy

Daniel Denison

Robert Hooijberg

Nancy Lane

Colleen Lief

Foreword by Edgar H. Schein

JOSSEY-BASS
A Wiley Imprint
www.josseybass.com

Published by Jossey-Bass
A Wiley Imprint
One Montgomery Street, Suite 1200, San Francisco, CA 94104-4594—www.josseybass.com

Cover art is by Thinkstock (RF.)

Jossey-Bass books and products are available through most bookstores. To contact Jossey-Bass directly call our Customer Care Department within the U.S. at 800-956-7739, outside the U.S. at 317-572-3986, or fax 317-572-4002.

Wiley publishes in a variety of print and electronic formats and by print-on-demand. Some material included with standard print versions of this book may not be included in e-books or in print-on-demand. If this book refers to media such as a CD or DVD that is not included in the version you purchased, you may download this material at http://booksupport.wiley.com. For more information about Wiley products, visit www.wiley.com.

Library of Congress Cataloging-in-Publication Data
Leading culture change in global organizations : aligning culture and strategy / Daniel Denison . . . [et al.] ; foreword by Edgar H. Schein.—1st ed.
    p. cm. —(J-B US non-franchise leadership ; 394)
    Includes bibliographical references and index.
  ISBN 978-0-470-90884-6 (hardback); ISBN 978-1-118-25967-2 (ebk);
ISBN 978-1-118-23510-2 (ebk); ISBN 978-1-118-22124-2 (ebk)
    1. Organizational behavior—Case studies. 2. Organizational change—Case studies.
3. Corporate culture—Case studies. 4. International business enterprises—Case studies.
I. Denison, Daniel R.
  HD58.7.L397 2012
  658.4'02—dc23

                                                                    2012015526

Printed in the United States of America
FIRST EDITION
HB Printing 10 9 8 7 6 5 4 3 2 1

Contents

Foreword

Much has happened in the field of organizational culture since the concept became theoretically and practically important in the 1980s. There were arguments about how to define it, how to measure it, and whether it was useful either as a construct in organization theory or as a correlate of organizational performance. The concept appealed to entrepreneurs because they saw themselves as creators of culture without always knowing just what they meant by that. The concept became important to leaders as a way of capturing all the soft stuff that they realized they had to think about and as a way of articulating their values. The concept played an increasing role in change theories, both as the biggest constraint on change and also as an element that had to change if real change were to be accomplished. The concept caught the fancy of theoreticians, who created instant typologies of different kinds of cultures. And the concept was immediately adopted by a number of social psychologists who wanted to measure it—whatever "it" was.

Among the early "measurers" was Dan Denison. His first culture book, *Corporate Culture and Organizational Effectiveness* (1990), showed that culture measures did relate to performance. In this new book, Denison and his colleagues have brought that whole approach to maturity and thereby have established a milestone in the culture studies arena. Through an analysis of a number of case studies of real culture change, they provide the reader with a useful and relevant measurement tool—built on relevant organization theory in its choice of dimensions to measure—and, most important, they show how the whole survey process integrates with an ongoing process of change.

The case studies show how working with culture both quantitatively and clinically can become the key to the major strategic and tactical change programs that organizations have to undertake in this ever more turbulent world. The book illustrates how effective culture measures have evolved and can be used creatively and responsibly. I say *responsibly*, because I have always been critical of those who used culture surveys when they simply assumed that they knew what to measure in the first place and then fed the results back to the organization without considering how this might help or hinder what the organization was trying to do.

What is presented in this book has come a long way from those early simplistic approaches. From the beginning, Denison was concerned with correlating culture dimensions with organizational performance, to impose a useful context for culture analysis. Culture is vast, but only some parts of a given organizational culture may be of relevance to what the organization is trying to do. And only some parts of culture connect with relevant organizational theories about how organizations could and should work. So Denison wisely chose to measure only those parts of culture that should relate to performance and has shown how the combination of measurement and working with the organization does indeed improve performance.

Developing a measurement tool, even with the right culture variables, is, of course, not nearly enough. Denison and his colleagues show us throughout how measuring culture elements is truly useful in helping organizations improve only if the measurement process itself becomes a useful intervention in the organization's own change process. A change-oriented leader cannot produce change without measurement tools, but a measurement-oriented leader cannot produce change without a strategy that integrates the measurement into the fabric of the change process. This is not easy to do, yet the cases analyzed here show the way.

By looking at the culture analysis over time, we gain both some sense of how valid the measurement tool is and, more important, what it actually takes to create organizational improvement, by showing how the measures focused the change activity. This commitment to measurement over time is an important aspect of what Denison and his team have shown to be essential in a change process. In illustrating how the variables measured change over time, the authors also show us important elements of organizational theory—what does it actually take to make cultural changes that matter? How do the choices of what we measure influence our theoretical thinking about what it takes to produce change?

These cases and the analysis will be of great use to researchers, consultants, and leaders who face the difficult problem of how to get culture change started and how to keep it on track.

Edgar H. Schein
professor emeritus,
MIT Sloan School of Management

To those who matter most. Our families: Graciela, Roland, Mia, Dakota, Brenda, Marta, Brianna, Pascal, Raphaël, Emmanuel, Eric, and Jasmine

Preface

The idea for this book first came up in a discussion that Robert Hooijberg and I had in 2009 while we were preparing a program stream for the International Institute for Management Development's (IMD) flagship executive program, Orchestrating Winning Performance (OWP). Each year in June, OWP brings together nearly five hundred executives at our campus in Lausanne, Switzerland. The IMD faculty are all in town to present their newest and best ideas, and this combination creates a lot of excitement and learning. That year, Robert and I had the opportunity to create a weeklong sequence of half-day sessions that we decided to title "Leading Culture Change in Global Organizations."

We had both worked for years with organizations as they tried to carry out significant culture changes. Some were a lot more successful than others! We had written a set of case studies, and we became especially interested in the group of companies in which we had tracked a successful set of changes over time using our Organizational Culture Survey. We knew the stories well, because we had worked with them closely throughout the change process. When we started to add up the possibilities, we quickly realized that we had a lot of global diversity: Domino's in the United States, Swiss Re from Switzerland, DeutscheTech from Germany, GT Automotive from the UK and the United States, Polar Bank from Scandinavia, GE Healthcare from China, and Vale from Brazil. All were global organizations, but they were looking at the cultural challenges of globalization from very different perspectives.

We managed to convince several of the executives from these companies to join us as guest speakers at OWP that year, and that gave us the opportunity to prepare several more teaching cases on these firms. Our coauthors Nancy Lane and Colleen Lief both began their involvement with this book project by writing teaching cases on several of these firms to prepare for their presentations at IMD. Everything went well at the OWP sessions. But as things were winding down after the program, we realized that we were on to something good. It was time to start writing this book.

With lots of good suggestions from Kathe Sweeney, our editor at Jossey-Bass/Wiley, we put together our plan of action. The chapters in this book cover a rich set of culture topics: the importance of supporting the front line, the dynamics of creating strategy alignment, the challenges of cultural integration in mergers and acquisitions, the process of importing culture change from one country to another, the lessons from building a global business *in* an emerging market, and the lessons from building a global business *from* an emerging market. Each of these topics is the focus of a chapter, and the company examples are used as cases. The survey results that we followed over time helped to ensure that we were on the right track in describing a change that, in the eyes of the organization's members, really made a difference.

The leaders of these organizations are the heroes in this book. We played an active role in these stories, and we are proud that most of these organizations would say that we helped them a lot. But the best parts of these stories are always the actions that the leaders took to transform their organizations by positioning the culture of the organization as a key part of the change process. This book is written for those leaders who are trying to manage their own organizations and want to learn more about how the culture of the firm can be an important point of leverage.

In this book we also aspire to make a practical contribution to the research literature. Since the beginning of the academic discussion of the importance of corporate culture, there has always been an emphasis on the deeper levels of culture that are hard for us to see—and even harder to change. Ed Schein explained all of this to us years ago: the importance of distinguishing the underlying assumptions from values and behaviors, or superficial artifacts. But it is still always difficult for us mere mortals to see these levels in practice. It's especially hard when we keep looking for a fundamental set of underlying assumptions that form the foundation of an organization's culture.

But at the end of this book, as we started to summarize what we had learned, we realized that a lot of the challenge of the change process involved changing rituals, habits, and routines. Habits have deep structures too and are hard to change, but they also have a fairly narrow bandwidth compared to the broad-based fundamentals that make up the set of underlying assumptions that culture researchers have been examining for years with limited success. Some were good habits, some were bad; some were old habits, and some were new. This insight led us to start looking at the organizations that we studied as interesting bundles of these interconnected habits. All of these habits had their roots in underlying assumptions, all were anchored in the value systems of their organizations, and all were manifested in a visible set of behaviors. As we worked with several companies to help them understand the cultural transformations that they were going through, we also found out that this framework was very useful. There's lots of work to do to develop this set of ideas for culture researchers, but this approach has already proven to be helpful in action.

The challenge of building a positive culture in a global organization is a daunting task. It is humbling to contemplate the scale and scope of the challenge, but inspiring to see what can be accomplished once things get started. We have had the privilege, in our careers, of watching a number of global companies try to pull this off. We hope that we have captured some of those lessons for you, so that you can help us put those ideas in action.

1

BUILDING A HIGH-PERFORMANCE BUSINESS CULTURE

Every human organization creates a unique culture all its own. From a small family business operating in its hometown, to a large global corporation spanning national cultures and time zones, each organization has a distinct identity. Tribes, families, cults, teams, and corporations all develop a complex and unique identity that evolves as they grow through the years.

Their culture always reflects the collective wisdom that comes from the lessons people learn as they adapt and survive together over time. Thousands of interlocking routines knit together the fabric of the firm and translate timeless knowledge into timely action on a daily basis. The traditional habits and customs that have kept the firm alive and well over time speak loud and clear. And when uncertainty rears its ugly head, the culture rules! All members of the corporate tribe tend to fall back on their tried-and-true methods in order to weather the storm.

Yet try as we might to look to the future, the knowledge embedded in our corporate cultures is always *yesterday's* knowledge, developed to meet the challenges of the past. What part of the past should we preserve for the future? How should we adapt the principles of the past to address the problems of the future? How should we go about the delicate task of relegating the obsolete practices of the past to the "corporate museum" so that they don't grow into obstacles that hold back our best practices and frustrate our best customers?

Some leaders try to ignore these challenges and concentrate on their expense ratios, analyst reports, discounted cash flows, and their next acquisition. Bad idea. Other top executives see shaping and managing the corporate culture as one of their most important challenges. As Wells Fargo Bank CEO John Stumpf said, "It's about the culture. I could leave our strategy on an airplane seat and have a competitor read it and it would not make any difference."[1] Former IBM Chairman Lou Gerstner made the same point: "Culture isn't just one aspect of the game—it *is* the game. In the end, an organization is no more than the collective capacity of its people to create value."[2] The people make the place.[3] The people create the organization. The people create the technology. The people organize the funding. The people develop the markets. Without implementation and alignment, there is no strategy, only a plan.

It can be easy to forget that the people make the place, because the structures that we create often outlive our memory of how and why we created them to begin with, leaving us feeling like we are the victims rather than the visionaries of the systems that we create. But over the long haul, one of the most powerful things that a company's leaders can do is to create a unique character and personality for their organization that fits their business environment and distinguishes them from the competition.

But where do you start? Research over the past two or three decades has shown that an organization's culture has an impact on business performance in four main ways:

- Creating an organization's sense of *mission* and direction
- Building a high level of *adaptability* and flexibility
- Nurturing the *involvement* and engagement of their people
- Providing a *consistency* that is strongly rooted in a set of core values

These are the cultural traits that most clearly affect business performance, so this is where the journey must begin.

But can something as complex as corporate culture actually be managed? The task is daunting—but doing nothing is not an attractive option! Organizational culture guru Edgar Schein said it best: "Either you manage the culture, or it manages you."[4] Managing culture change is certainly not easy, but there are plenty of real-life examples of global companies who have succeeded. This book is built around seven of those examples.

What Is Corporate Culture? Why Is It Important?

At the climax of the annual holiday party of one rapidly growing American company, hundreds of balloons are released from the ceiling. Inside each balloon is a crisp new US$100 bill. Whoever scrambles the hardest gets the most money! The lesson is simple, fun, and more powerful than all the personnel policy handbooks in the world. It helps capture the essence of some of the key definitions of corporate culture: Culture is both "the way we do things around here" and "what we do when we think no one is looking." Culture is "the code, the core logic, the software of the mind that organizes the behavior of the people," and "the lessons that we have learned that are important enough to pass on to the next generation."[5]

Schein's classic approach divides culture into three levels.[6] He argues that basic underlying assumptions lie at the root of culture and are "unconscious, taken-for-granted beliefs, perceptions, thoughts, and feelings." Espoused values are derived from the basic underlying assumptions and are the "espoused justifications of strategies, goals and philosophies." Finally, at the top level are "artifacts," defined as the "visible, yet hard to decipher organizational structures and processes."

Consider the iceberg image presented in Figure 1.1. Only about 10 percent of an iceberg is visible above the water; 90 percent is below the surface. But the *inertia* of the part that is beneath the surface is what will sink your ship. Similarly, it is often the parts of the culture that we *can't* see that will get us into

Figure 1.1. Culture Reflects the Lessons Learned Over Time

Visible Symbols

Survival

Culture

Underlying Principles

Lessons

Artifacts, behaviors, and norms are visible and tangible

Personal values and attitudes are less visible, but can be talked about

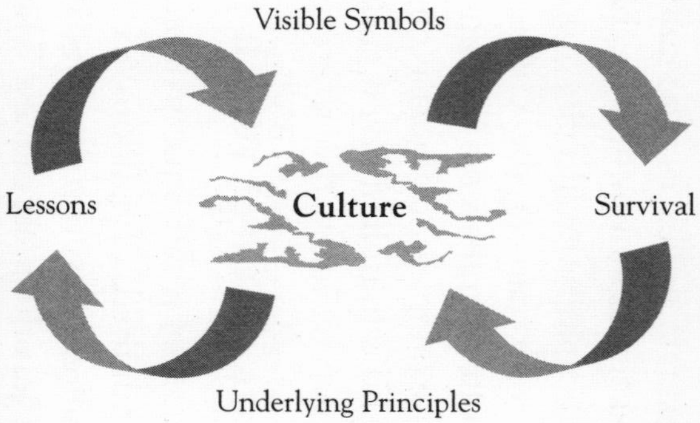

Underlying beliefs and assumptions are subconscious, invisible, and rarely questioned

trouble. This figure also reminds us that the culture is learned—it is built up from the accumulated principles that we learn as we survive together over time. The lessons from the past shape our survival strategies for the future. Winston Churchill said something similar about architecture: "We shape our buildings; thereafter they shape us."[7]

So our mindset and worldview shape the way that we use the lessons of the past to forge the strategies of the future. How well are business leaders doing? Well, the record is not all that encouraging. Phil Rosenzweig's best seller *The Halo Effect*[8] explains that when successful corporations become legends, their business practices are imitated for both good reasons and bad. Neither researchers nor executives have done particularly well at separating the principles and practices that truly impact business performance from those that are simply imitated because a corporation enjoyed great success and everyone now wants to be like them. Telling fashion from function is often harder than it looks.

There's a long tradition of studying "superstitious learning," which probably has its roots in Malinowski's study of the "cargo cult" of the Trobriand Islanders in Papua New Guinea nearly one hundred years ago.[9] Richard Feynman tells the story with an example from the end of World War II:

> During the war they saw airplanes land with lots of good materials, and they want the same thing to happen now. So they've arranged to imitate things like runways, to put fires along the sides of the runways, to make a wooden hut for a man to sit in, with two wooden pieces on his head like headphones and bars of bamboo sticking out like antennas—he's the controller—and they wait for the airplanes to land. They're doing everything right. The form is perfect. It looks exactly the way it looked before. But it doesn't work. No airplanes land.[10]

You may be thinking "Surely modern corporate 'tribes' must do far better at separating fact from fiction and deciding what really works than the ancient tribes of Papua New Guinea!" Well, let's not jump to conclusions. Many of the recent accounts of the subprime mortgage crisis emphasize the growing power of the system that was created.[11] Mortgage loan officers made a bigger bonus if they booked more subprime loans. Fee income from new loans was high enough that even bad loans were good business for the banks. These government-guaranteed loans were sold to other banks, who created securities that were certified AAA grade. Investors around the world grabbed these up because they paid a higher rate of return. This system created an insatiable demand for banks to find even more prospective buyers who would borrow beyond their means in hopes of "flipping" their new home to take advantage of rising real estate prices before their balloon payment came due. This system paid off so well that in the short term everyone kept looking for the next deal long after the system had stopped paying off. Thus we see how ritual can become separated from reality even in the most sophisticated organizations.[12]

How Corporate Culture Impacts Business Performance

Over the past twenty years, we've studied the link between organizational culture and business performance. We've been trying to understand the cultural traits that explain the difference between high- and low-performing organizations.[13] These studies have examined the link between the four basic traits in our model—*mission, adaptability, involvement,* and *consistency*—and performance measures such as profitability, sales growth, quality, innovation, and market value. Out of this research, we've developed a way to measure culture, and we've created a widely used Culture Survey designed to help organizations focus on the issues that need attention and move beyond a discussion of employee satisfaction, engagement, and morale, to better understand the actions they can take to build their organizations for the future. Figure 1.2 shows what we've found out about "What Counts."

• *Mission.* Successful organizations have a clear sense of purpose and direction that allows them to define organizational goals and strategies and to create a compelling vision of the organization's future. Leaders play a critical role in defining mission, but a mission can only be reached if it is well understood, top to bottom. A clear mission provides purpose and meaning by defining a compelling social role and a set of goals for the organization. We focus on three aspects of mission: *strategic direction and intent, goals and objectives,* and *vision.*

• *Adaptability.* A strong sense of purpose and direction must be complemented by a high degree of flexibility and responsiveness to the business environment. Organizations with a strong sense of purpose and direction often are the least adaptive and the most difficult to change. Adaptable organizations, in contrast, quickly translate the demands of the organizational environment into action. We focus on three dimensions of adaptability: *creating change, customer focus,* and *organizational learning.*

• *Involvement.* Effective organizations empower and engage their people, build their organization around teams, and develop human capability at all levels. Organizational members are highly committed to their work and feel a strong sense of engagement and ownership. People at all levels feel that they have input into the decisions that affect their work and feel that their work is directly connected to the goals of the organization. We focus on three characteristics of involvement: *empowerment, team orientation,* and *capability development.*

• *Consistency.* Organizations are most effective when they are consistent and well integrated. Behavior must be rooted in a set of core values, and people must be skilled at putting these values into action by reaching agreement while incorporating

Figure 1.2. What Counts

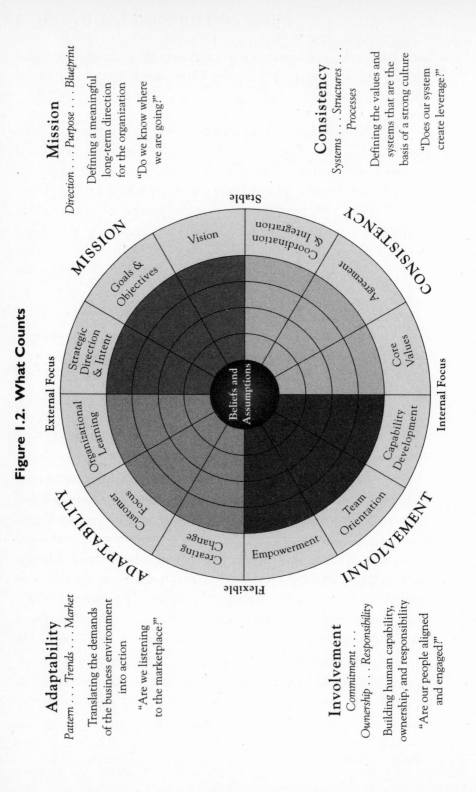

Mission

Direction . . . Purpose . . . Blueprint

Defining a meaningful long-term direction for the organization

"Do we know where we are going?"

Consistency

Systems . . . Structures . . . Processes

Defining the values and systems that are the basis of a strong culture

"Does our system create leverage?"

Adaptability

Pattern . . . Trends . . . Market

Translating the demands of the business environment into action

"Are we listening to the marketplace?"

Involvement

Commitment . . . Ownership . . . Responsibility

Building human capability, ownership, and responsibility

"Are our people aligned and engaged?"

diverse points of view. These organizations have highly commit-ted employees, a distinct method of doing business, a tendency to promote from within, and a clear set of do's and don'ts. This type of consistency is a powerful source of stability and internal integra-tion. We focus on three consistency factors: *core values*, *agreement*, and *coordination and integration*.

Like many contemporary models of leadership and organi-zational effectiveness, this model focuses on a set of dynamic contradictions or tensions that must be managed.[14] As Schein and others have noted, effective cultures always need to solve two problems at the same time: external adaptation and internal inte-gration. Four tensions are highlighted by the model: the trade-off between stability and flexibility and the trade-off between inter-nal and external focus are the basic underlying dimensions of the framework.[15] In addition, the diagonal tensions between internal consistency and external adaptability, and the "top-down" versus "bottom-up" tension between mission and involvement exem-plify some of the competing demands that organizations face.

For each of these dynamic contradictions, it is relatively easy to do one or the other, but much more difficult to do both. Organi-zations that are market focused and aggressive in pursuing every opportunity often have the most trouble with internal inte-gration. Organizations that are extremely well integrated and controlled often have the hardest time focusing on the customer. Organizations with the most powerful top-down vision often find it difficult to focus on the bottom-up dynamics needed to implement that vision. Effective organizations, however, find a way to resolve these dynamic contradictions without relying on a simple trade-off. American novelist F. Scott Fitzgerald expressed the same concept when he said that "the test of a first rate intelligence is the ability to hold two contradictory ideas at the same time and still retain the capability to function."[16]

At the core of this model we find underlying beliefs and assumptions. Although these deeper levels of organizational culture are difficult to measure, they provide the foundation from which behavior and action spring. Basic beliefs and assumptions about the organization and its people, the customer, the marketplace and the industry, and the basic value proposition of the firm create a tightly knit logic that holds the organization together. But when organizations are facing change or encountering new challenges from the competition, this core set of beliefs and assumptions, and the strategies and structures that are built on this foundation, come under fire. When that happens, the organizational system and the culture that holds it together need to be reexamined.

Some Real Examples

The concepts in this model were developed by listening to hundreds of stories from organizations large and small, public and private, old and new, successful and unsuccessful, all over the world. To illustrate how central these four traits are to real-world business success, let's now consider four well-known examples: IKEA, Apple, Ritz-Carlton, and Toyota.

IKEA: Mission Grows Out of Core Beliefs and Assumptions

IKEA founder Ingwar Kamprad grew up in the hardscrabble farmlands of southern Sweden and became an entrepreneur at an early age. By 1976, well established in the Swedish furniture business, he summarized his key principles of doing business in a little book called *A Furniture Dealer's Testament*.[17] It is remarkable how many of the principles described in this book are still alive at IKEA over thirty years later.

Like most great organizations, Kamprad's company has not just produced profits but has also tried to serve a higher purpose in the world. IKEA brings style, value, and a better life to many.

The company's products are designed for the global everyman, combining frugality, innovation, and style, using environmentally friendly materials. Everyone deserves the opportunity to be part of the IKEA revolution.

> What is good for our customers is also, in the long run, good for us. This is an objective that carries obligations.... The objective must be to encompass the total home environment; that is, to offer furnishings and fittings for every part of the home whether indoors or outdoors.... It must reflect our way of thinking by being as simple and straightforward as we are ourselves. It must be durable and easy to live with. It must reflect an easier, more natural, and unconstrained way of life.[18]

In his book, Kamprad also expressed strong beliefs about how IKEA should operate, stressing the simplicity and self-reliance of an individual who today is worth over $30 billion but still counts every penny like it was his last. Consider his thoughts on simplicity:

> Bureaucracy complicates and paralyzes! Exaggerated planning is the most common cause of corporate death. We do not need fancy cars, posh titles, tailor-made uniforms or other status symbols. We rely on our strength and our will.[19]

IKEA is a terrific example of how a global business strategy can grow from the core beliefs and assumptions of the founder. Consider just one key element of the IKEA system: the *flatpack*. As all loyal IKEA shoppers know, after following the one-way corridor through the store, looking at the kitchens and the bedrooms, and stopping at the restaurant for a coffee or light meal, you eventually make your way to checkout and finally pick up your purchases. They are all packed in flat boxes designed to take home and assemble yourself. You get the home entertainment at no extra charge!

Where did this brilliant strategic innovation come from? Was it the result of an expensive study from a leading consultancy? Or an outgrowth of a corporate innovation center designed to make IKEA more customer centric? No way!

In 1952, one of IKEA's first employees, Gillis Lundgren, had a problem. He was trying to load a table into his Volvo to deliver to a customer. It didn't fit. Gillis thought, "God, what a lot of space that takes up! Let's take the legs off and put them under the table top."[20] Voilà! Global strategy. The rest is just implementation. By 1956, this practice was standardized and has been an essential part of the IKEA experience ever since. The current system has continued to build on these key principles established in the early days.

IKEA's strong sense of mission and powerful corporate culture are not without their limitations. Growth has been steady, but relatively slow, especially given the dramatic enthusiasm of their customers. IKEA has never made much of an impact in the office furniture market, mostly because very few corporations want to assemble their own office furniture. Expanding to countries that are farther and farther away from their Swedish homeland has also presented some challenges. Successful franchisees who do like "fancy cars, posh titles, tailor-made uniforms, or other status symbols," have also posed difficult choices for IKEA. But overall, "The IKEA Way" has been a central part of the fifty-year journey from an entrepreneur's dream to a global icon.

Apple: Adaptability Leads the Marketplace into the Future

Since Apple's founding in 1976 in a garage in Cupertino, California, its people have built their success around an unparalleled understanding of their customers' tacit needs. They deliver their technology to their customers in a way that shapes the customers' desires. Time and again, they have developed new products that their customers didn't really know they needed until they found out that they couldn't live without them. As cofounder Steve

Jobs put it, Apple has focused their attention on developing "toys for yuppies," while their competitors were often focused on the MHz of their new CPUs.[21]

A powerful recent example of Apple's genius in leading the marketplace is the App Store. It is a fascinating example of the competitive advantage created by adaptability. Building on their spectacular success with the iPod and iTunes, Apple set about developing the hardware and software to create another new market that didn't exist before: the smartphone and the App Store.

Nearly a half billion iPods later, it is hard to believe that ten years ago no one had ever heard of an iPod. A few of us downloaded digital music, but most of us were still carrying around CDs. But the iPod quickly became a necessity for people all over the world. Apple created a fundamental innovation in the way that music was delivered to consumers, building a new platform for revenue generation and innovation that would carry the firm far into the future. Apple was the intermediary between consumers and the music that they love.

This set the stage for Apple's entry into the smartphone business with the launch of the first iPhone in June 2007. The iPhone turned the iPod into a touchscreen cellphone with internet access. No longer would people need to carry a phone and an iPod and still find themselves in need of access to the internet to look up movie times or restaurant locations. Now it was all in the palm of their hand. And it was a big bet that the future of cellphones would be differentiated not by "radios and attennas and things like that," but instead by software.[22] The bet paid off handsomely—by Q4 2008 Apple surpassed BlackBerry maker Research in Motion to become the world's third largest phone maker, after Nokia and Samsung.

At first, developers created their own unsanctioned apps. But in March 2008, Apple released a software development kit to help developers create their own apps. They also created a radical set of rules for the App Store.[23] It would cost developers $99 to submit an app, and they could charge whatever they wanted for downloads. Apple would retain 30 percent of the sale price for administration. The remaining 70 percent would go to the developer. If the app were offered for free, Apple would take no commission. Apple itself would maintain the App Store, control the approval process, and support the whole thing through iTunes.

The App Store was launched with five hundred apps in July 2008, to coincide with the global launch of the 3G iPhone in twenty-two countries. In the first year, nearly one hundred thousand apps were created, with two billion downloads to over twenty million iPhones worldwide. By the time that this book is published, there will be over one million apps. Apple now estimates that the App Store generates more than $1 billion each year.

Apple's approach to innovation is deeply rooted in their DNA. It has always been informed by a unique mindset that focuses on the *ecosystem* that surrounds their customers. Their innovations combine hardware and software with developers and consumers in ways that create revolutionary markets. The App Store connects the endless creativity of the developers with consumers' endless demand for software solutions, starting at a price point of $.99 or less and building from there. With Apple as the intermediary, Steve Jobs's legacy of innovation will be with us for a long time to come.

Ritz-Carlton Hotels: Involvement Creates Capacity

Ritz-Carlton hotels founder Cesar Ritz set the luxury standard for European hotels in the early twentieth century. He said, "Never say no when a client asks for something, even if they ask for the moon. You can always try." Ritz-Carlton's "Three Steps of Service" set a high standard for five-star quality:

1. A warm and sincere greeting. Use the guest's name.
2. Anticipation and fulfillment of each guest's needs.
3. A fond farewell. Give a warm good-bye and use the guest's name.

The Ritz-Carlton refers to their twenty-eight thousand people as "ladies and gentlemen, serving ladies and gentlemen." Their remarkable core values are well understood by their people, starting with the "Employee Promise" and the "Credo."

But perhaps the most remarkable part of all of this is what it takes to actually do this: every day, all of the Ritz-Carlton ladies and gentlemen participate in a daily briefing. All of their service people, in all of their hotels, meet to discuss the incidents that arose through the day, the actions that they took to address them, and how those fit with the Ritz-Carlton principles. This debrief is led by the local manager. The day's incidents and actions are also captured in their system so that they have a record of every guest's experience in each stay. That record can be used to anticipate and accommodate a guest's experience, even if it is at another Ritz-Carlton hotel. This allows the staff to achieve an unusual mark of distinction: they can create the same level of customer service for each of their clients at each hotel. The preferences that are established for a client at one hotel can be applied across the country or around the world at any time.

A friend of mine tells a story of going out for a run while staying at a Ritz-Carlton hotel. The first time, when he came back after the run, they asked him if he wanted something to drink. He asked for a bottle of water. The second time they had a bottle of water ready for him, and asked him if he preferred sparkling or still water! To his amazement, this knowledge of his personal habits and preferences followed him on to his next stay at another Ritz-Carlton hotel.

We usually associate high-involvement work practices with flat, democratic organizations with few levels and few status distinctions. But this is one part of the Ritz-Carlton culture that makes it an intriguing example: in order to thrive with a demanding clientele in a luxury segment of the market, they stake their claim on bottom-up input! And they do walk the talk: each of the "ladies and gentlemen" in their service operation has the authority to spend $2,500 on the spot to resolve a guest's concerns.

Some might argue that you can afford to lavish such attention on customers only when you are operating in a luxury segment of the market like the one that Ritz-Carlton serves.[24] The average annual income of their guests is over $250,000, and nearly half of their guests are repeat visitors. Clearly, it is a big business decision to invest the time of both the managers and the staff in the daily debrief. But without this key part of the process, the good ideas would just remain good ideas. They wouldn't be put into action as the cornerstone of a time-tested competitive strategy that differentiates a Ritz-Carlton hotel from the rest of the pack in the luxury segment.

Toyota: Consistency Is the Foundation for Quality

Toyota was created by the Toyoda Automatic Loom Works in 1937 to produce automobiles. Their early history was one of difficult struggle, which required them to take advantage of every opportunity they could find to reduce waste and use resources efficiently. Toyota's culture grew organically for many years before the company attracted much attention. But by the 1980s, their world-class quality and conspicuous success led many to try to capture their essence and understand the huge leaps in competitive advantage that Toyota had made on the rest of the manufacturing world. Today, the Toyota Way is one of the most clearly articulated management philosophies in the world—there is probably more written about Toyota than about any other company, with the possible exception of General Electric.[25] But, as many companies have found when trying to imitate the Toyota Production System, it is much easier to describe the Toyota mindset and culture than it is to copy it. To quote Toyota's former president, Fujio Cho:

> The key to the Toyota Way and what makes Toyota stand out is not any of the individual elements. But what is important is having all the elements together as a system. It must be practiced every day in a very consistent manner, not in spurts.

We place highest value on actual implementation and taking action. There are many things one doesn't understand and therefore, we ask them, why don't you just go ahead and take action; try to do something? You realize how little you know and face your own failures and you simply can correct those failures and redo it again and at the second trial you realize another mistake or another thing you didn't like so you can redo it once again. So by constant improvement, or, should I say, the improvement based upon action, one can rise to the higher level of practice and knowledge.[26]

There are fourteen different elements to the Toyota Way that have been clearly articulated in many different sources. One of the key factors is the reliance on "pull" systems that avoid overproduction and force the organization and its supply chain to respond to the market demands. This helps them to create a continuous process flow that brings problems to the surface, levels out the workload, and forces them to stop to fix problems so that they can get quality right the first time. This approach is also extended to their partners and suppliers by challenging them and helping them improve.

Toyota's system has been built from their experience, over time. Toyota develops leaders who thoroughly understand the work and live the philosophy. They rely on "visual" controls so that no problems are hidden, and when there are problems, they encourage leaders to "go and see for themselves." Finally, they base their management decisions on a long-term philosophy; they make decisions slowly through consensus but then implement them rapidly. They have led the way in their industry in resolving the dynamic paradox between internal consistency and external adaptability. They have done this by becoming a learning organization that has mastered relentless reflection and continuous improvement.

Each of these principles is significant in its own right and is a required part of the overall system. It is a system created to manage complexity in an efficient and predictable way through nearly flawless lateral coordination. Nonetheless, it can also be relatively simple once you develop the mindset that allows you to see the flow.[27] "All we are doing is looking at the time line from the moment the customer gives us an order to the point when we collect the cash. And we are reducing that time line by removing the non-value-added wastes."[28]

Toyota has successfully transplanted the logic and culture of their production system all over the world. This evolving philosophy has led Toyota from its original position as a struggling automaker in pre-war Japan to that of the largest and most profitable automotive company in the world. Moreover, Toyota manufacturing methods are imitated by nearly every manufacturer in the world in hopes of reaching the levels of quality and consistency defined by the leader.

But in early 2010, Toyota faced their biggest challenge in years. "Sudden acceleration" problems with Toyota vehicles in North America made headlines all over the world and compromised their reputation. Overnight, their stock price and sales dropped dramatically. Even though the technical issues that are at the heart of this problem have proven surprisingly difficult to establish, one strong lesson does emerge from this case: when your reputation is built on quality and consistency, it is absolutely necessary to protect and defend that characteristic in order to preserve and, as necessary, rebuild your brand. When we claim to live by our core values, people expect us to live up to them every day, without fail.

These examples—IKEA, Apple, Ritz-Carlton, and Toyota— were all chosen to illustrate the importance of the principles of mission, adaptability, involvement, and consistency. They are all remarkable success stories that show the power of these principles and help to illustrate what these principles mean in practical business terms.

Leading Culture Change in Global Organizations

This book tries to address a big void in the literature about culture and leadership in organizations: What happens when you try to change organizations? What works? What doesn't? Is it all chance and charisma? Or is it all process, methods, measures, and structure? Many authors have given us great principles for leading change in organizations.[29] But very few have tried to systematically track what works and what doesn't so that we can learn more about how to create successful change in global organizations.

Again, we have built this book around a set of seven case studies from all over the world in which we have tracked organizations and their leaders over time, studied the changes that they have made, and tried to understand the impact that those changes have had on the business. For each organization, we analyzed "before and after" survey results to track the culture change. This assessment is a central part of this book, and we use this same approach in each chapter to track the progress that each organization is making. So let's take a minute to look at one brief example and learn how to interpret these profiles.

The four concepts in the culture model are measured through a sixty-item survey that produces a profile. This profile compares the results to a benchmark database of over a thousand organizations.[30] These sixty items measure the four culture traits of mission, adaptability, involvement, and consistency. Each of these four traits is measured with three indexes, and each of those twelve indexes is measured using five survey items. This analysis helps to identify the strengths and weaknesses of the organization's culture and understand the impact that it may be having on business performance. For those with more interest in this survey and the research that supports it, we have included a detailed discussion in the Appendix, including an example that shows the sixty items that make up the twelve indexes.

The first rule for interpreting a culture profile is simple: *more color is better*. The scores on the profile show where the organization ranks relative to the benchmark. For example, a score of 9 on *vision* means that the organization ranks in the 9th percentile, telling them that 91 percent of the other companies in the benchmark database scored higher than they did on vision.

When the executive team of the One-Hundred-Year-Old Manufacturing Company looked at their results (see Figure 1.3), there was a long silence. The president, who had spent his career in operations, said, "Well, I admit that I'm not a visionary or a strategist—I'm the guy who makes the trains run on time." When they focused on the results for consistency, they agreed that their emphasis on internal control made it difficult to react to the marketplace. They agreed that they had strong core values, but they also questioned whether they were the right core values for the future. One of them spoke up: "Our core values are perfectly suited for meeting the challenges of the 1980s." Finally, when

Figure 1.3. The One-Hundred-Year-Old Manufacturing Company

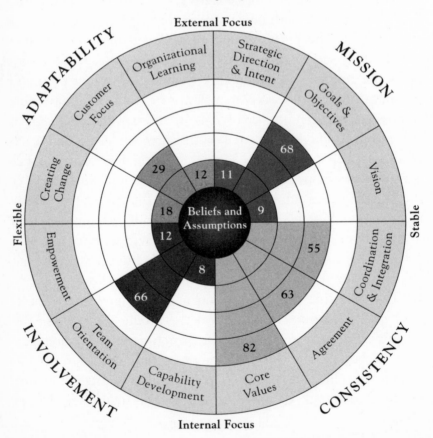

they looked at their results on team orientation, one of them concluded, "We're a team all right—we're all going down together!"

These results helped this leadership team see that the system they had created made it hard to innovate and grow, even though they still produced excellent quality products and were a good employer for many of their people. But the results also helped convince the leadership team that they were at the center of the problem and that their actions had to be at the center of any solution.

When confronted with this kind of result, most organizations that carry out successful changes go through a change process that looks something like the process depicted in Figure 1.4. The

Figure 1.4. Leading Culture Change

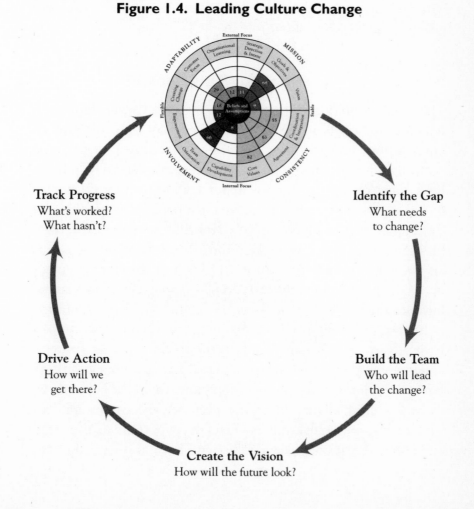

Track Progress
What's worked?
What hasn't?

Identify the Gap
What needs
to change?

Drive Action
How will we
get there?

Build the Team
Who will lead
the change?

Create the Vision
How will the future look?

survey results help to identify the gaps and define what needs to change. But to drive action, an organization needs to build a team—a "guiding coalition," in Harvard Professor John Kotter's terms—that will create a vision of the future, and define the actions and the accountabilities that will get them where they want to go.[31] A commitment to tracking progress is also important in order to bring some accountability to the change process. As noted management consultant Ram Charan put it, "There's a fine line between vision and hallucination."[32] Tracking progress usually leads to another round of focused change. Each of the organizations that we studied for this book has gone through some variation of this general change process. We were involved with the change process in each of these organizations and will give you an overview of our role in each chapter.

The Plan for This Book

This book is unique in that it is built around seven longitudinal case studies. We have followed the change process in each organization, and we have tracked that change process using "before-and-after" survey results over several years to help highlight some of the key lessons about leading culture change in global organizations. We start in Chapter Two by looking at the importance of supporting the frontline people in the organization, using the case of Domino's Pizza. Domino's presents an exciting story of the transition of a firm that had been led by its founder for nearly forty years, through a Bain Capital buyout, a new CEO, a successful IPO, and the implementation of a strategy based on people as the primary source of competitive advantage. Chapter Three turns to the topic of strategic alignment and uses the examples of two European organizations. First, the German technology company DeutscheTech shows us how a clear alignment of the purpose, vision, and strategy across organizational levels is critically important to the strategy implementation process. Chapter Three also examines the implementation of a crisis-driven top-down strategic change at Swiss Re's Americas Division. This example shows how changes that have a real impact on day-to-day work are the most likely to "stick" and to have a lasting effect. Chapter Four focuses on one of the most common topics in culture work: cultural integration in mergers and acquisitions. Although firms realize that it is hard to create scale without integration, they still struggle to get everyone around the world on the same page. This chapter focuses on Polar Bank, a Scandinavian bank trying to integrate three different acquisitions and make one culture out of many.

Chapter Five leads us to an even more complex topic: the exporting of culture change from the United States to Europe. GT Automotive, a UK-based firm, completes a successful transformation in their American division and then tries to export these changes back to their European organization. Chapter Six focuses on the challenge of building a global business in a developing market. We examine General Electric's efforts to build their health care business in China and then use that platform to build a global business. In our final case study, we focus on the challenges of creating a global corporation from a base in an emerging market by tracing the Brazilian mining company Vale in their ten-year journey from being a department in the Brazilian government to becoming a global player. In our final chapter, we summarize the key lessons for leaders about the magic and the method of these transformation stories. We discuss these lessons in terms of a new model of the rituals, habits, and routines that lie at the heart of their organizations' cultures.

Fasten your seat belts!

2

SUPPORTING THE FRONT LINE

Japanese scholar Ikujiro Nonaka first rose to fame in his home country with his analysis of the role of the U.S. Marines in the Pacific theater during World War II.[1] The Marines, he argued, were amphibious warriors, who moved from the sea onto the land with a discipline that the Japanese generals had never seen before. Nonaka seized on the critical importance of those who stormed the beaches first—the "gravel crunchers" as the Marines called them. It was a dangerous job. Even when the mission was "successful," the gravel crunchers could often end up dead, face down in the water, with tank tracks up their backs. But the tanks were on the beach! So in order to succeed, the Marines needed to make certain that they did everything that they could do to support the gravel crunchers, because they were "the sharp end of the spear"—if they didn't succeed, the entire mission would fail. This image teaches us the first lesson of building a successful corporate culture, especially in the service industry. Support the front line! Everything depends on their success and their survival.

JetBlue Airways learned this lesson the hard way. Their unique high-involvement culture and friendly customer service initially helped make them the fastest-growing airline in the competitive U.S. market. In 2006, for example, they set a record by opening fifteen new routes in an attempt to consolidate their position in the market. But this dramatic increase in traffic stretched their growing human and organizational infrastructure to the limit. On Valentine's Day 2007, they reached their limit.

In a fierce ice storm at New York's JFK International Airport, their operational infrastructure broke down, leaving passengers stranded on the runway for hours. The return to "normal" took three days, with the disruption continuing long after the ice storm had passed. JetBlue's well-deserved reputation and carefully crafted brand took a major beating in the media.

But rather than retrenching to a more traditional command-and-control structure, JetBlue's approach to solving this problem reinforced the unique high-involvement culture that had fueled their rapid growth in the first place. They didn't take a top-down approach to creating the infrastructure needed to recover from this operational setback. Instead, they brought together a broad, cross-functional coalition of frontline crew members. This team, with full support from the top, developed the JetBlue strategy for recovering from an interruption in service and solved this problem so that it would never happen again. And it hasn't.

Creating a system that supports the front line makes all the difference, no matter where you are in the world. The Chinese company Galanz, now the world's largest producer of microwave ovens, is built around teams, and they work hard to develop human capability at all levels. This is an important advantage in the hypercompetitive Chinese labor market. Galanz is run like a family, striving to develop a culture of emotional attachment between the company and its employees. Liang Qingde, the founder and chairman of Galanz, is called "Uncle De," and employees call each other "Brother X" or "Sister X" like they are a part of a family. At the end of each year, Uncle De writes a letter to all employees and their families, expressing appreciation for their work. Galanz's success in supporting their forty thousand employees helped them reach US$2 billion in revenue for 2008. Employees are supported in a very different way from how it might be done in a Western organization, but the effect is very similar.

The challenge of supporting the front line is important in all organizations, but it is especially important in service organizations, where the product is produced as it is delivered.

Whether your organization is a brokerage or a burger stand, a franchise or a fraternity, a hotel or a hospital, a college or consulting firm, you cannot function effectively without high-quality human interaction with your customers. Without the involvement of the front line, you can't really deliver the most important part of the organization's strategy: implementation. And as far as we can tell, the market doesn't pay many rewards to strategies that aren't well implemented. Without the right mindset and behavior on the front line, there is no strategy—only a set of unexecuted plans.

Making the Front Line the Foundation of Your Strategy

In this chapter, we focus on Domino's Pizza, which gives us an example of an organization that took a big step forward in quality and performance when they finally decided that they needed to make their people the foundation of their competitive strategy. We tracked this story very carefully over a number of years. So let's start from the beginning.

Domino's Pizza was founded in 1960 by two brothers, Tom and Jim Monaghan, who each kicked in $500 to buy a pizza shop. Before long, Jim wanted out, so he traded his half of the store to Tom in exchange for Tom's well-used Volkswagen Beetle. In his thirty-nine years of leading the company, Tom Monaghan transformed this one pizza delivery shop into one of the world's top brands. In 1999, with six thousand stores and over $3 billion in revenues, Monaghan sold 93 percent of the company to Bain Capital, which soon brought in David Brandon as CEO.[2]

How do you go about creating competitive advantage in the pizza delivery business? Is it the pepperoni? The cheese? Maybe the anchovies? The new CEO and his team made the decision that the only way to create competitive advantage in their business was through the *people*. In his first week on the job, Brandon learned that the annual staff turnover was 158 percent.

After doing the math, he realized that with 150,000 people, the company might have trouble finding enough time to make pizzas and deliver them if they had to continue hiring and training nearly a quarter of a million people each year. What stunned Brandon even more was the current HR leader's acceptance of this level of turnover as being "normal for this industry." Brandon soon recruited a new HR executive from outside the industry. She was Patti Wilmot, and she was ready for the challenge.

Brandon took over at Domino's after a career that started at Procter & Gamble on the recommendation of his football coach at the University of Michigan. He'd gone on to become the CEO of a direct marketing company, Valassis Communications, which he grew from a firm with a few hundred employees to a spot on *FORTUNE*'s 100 Best Places to Work list. Here's what he said to his people the first day on the job at Domino's:

> If you don't remember anything else about me today, just remember these three words—*Change is good*. Change is not a criticism of the past. It just means the future is going to be different. If that sounds exciting to you, you're going to love me. If any of you are thinking "I'd rather do things the way we've always done them," I've got to tell you—you're going to hate me.[3]

Whether he was leading several thousand Domino's people shouting out the Domino's vision—"We are exceptional people on a mission to be the best pizza delivery company in the world!"—or teaching finance to new store managers, or convincing skeptical industry analysts, Brandon always preached Domino's four guiding principles: "People First," "Build the Brand," "Maintain High Standards," and "Flawless Execution." Domino's staff had worked together to develop these guiding principles during the first year of the transformation.

They made every attempt to improve the quality of the workforce. Hiring placed more emphasis on attitude because they felt that skills could be taught, but attitude could be stubbornly permanent. Drug testing for delivery drivers, new financial software designed to prevent "shrinkage" and theft, and a ban on hiring former employees who had been fired were all implemented to help improve the quality of the workforce.

Each segment of the employee population received special attention. A "pipeline" was created for each segment that defined hiring criteria, developmental targets and investments, advancement opportunities, and exit plans. The pipeline was managed for all segments of the employee population, from pizza delivery boys to store managers and franchisees to future executives and board members. Poorly performing franchisees, in the bottom 25 percent, were also invited to "straight talk" sessions where they discussed their store's performance. Part of the discussion always focused on the business potential of a well-run franchise. If a franchisee would not devote the time and attention it took to be successful, Domino's was always ready to help them or to help broker a deal to sell their underperforming stores to another franchisee.

Domino's performance steadily improved. After their 2004 IPO, Bain Capital noted that Domino's was one of the best private equity deals that they had ever done, returning over 500 percent on their investment.[4] Involvement, capability, and teamwork were the hallmarks of their success.

Tracking the Progress

We tracked Domino's progress over five years, as this transformation unfolded. The tracking process was designed to make sure that the progress that the organization was making wasn't just in the minds of the executives in the C-suite, but that things were really starting to change on the ground. The survey was based upon our organizational culture model, and it included all of the levels of management as well as the people in the stores.

The baseline culture data from 2001 are presented in Figure 2.1. These results show that Domino's started with some

Figure 2.1. 2001 Culture Survey Results: Domino's Pizza

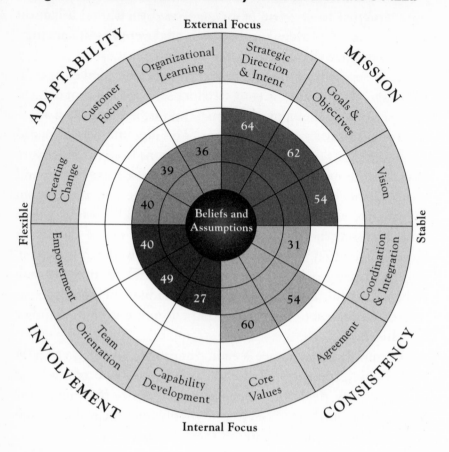

clear challenges: Capability Development, Coordination and Integration, Customer Focus, and Organizational Learning were all below the fortieth percentile when compared to the global benchmark.[5] The survey results also helped Brandon and his leadership team to clarify their goals for transforming the organization. The low scores in the involvement area—in capability development, in particular—confirmed that Domino's had their work cut out for them when it came to improving the capability of their people on the front line. These results in Figure 2.1 summarize the perspective of management as a whole. But when we looked in more detail at the lower levels of management and the people in the stores, the involvement scores are even lower. When Domino's compared their culture scores for the higher- and lower-performing stores and regions, they found that the culture at the region and store level also made a big difference.

They set goals to cut employee turnover in half and to be acknowledged as one of the one hundred best companies to work for in America. They also focused on a clear set of business goals, setting their target on being "Wall Street ready" so that they would be prepared for an IPO in the near future by hitting their targets of ten thousand stores and $200 million EBITDA (Earnings Before Interest, Taxes, Depreciation, and Amortization). The survey results from 2003 (Figure 2.2) show the progress that they had made. Domino's had taken big steps forward in the areas of Coordination and Integration, Customer Focus, Creating Change, and Capability Development. They were now at least slightly above average on everything, with real strengths in all areas of Mission. These results show the clear effects of two years of hard work in clarifying the direction of the organization and setting clear expectations about the level of ambition that was expected from the people.

But they didn't stop there. Their survey results from 2004, presented in Figure 2.3, show that they had continued to make forward progress as they drove the transformation deeper into the organization. The feedback about their progress and their challenges was shared widely in the company. and all of the managers involved went through a goal-setting process that they called SMAC. This involved discussing their results, linking them to the real business issues behind the results, and then creating a set of action steps that fit the SMAC criteria: the goals had to be *specific*, *measurable*, *achievable*, and *consistent* with the

Figure 2.2. Comparing 2001 to 2003 Culture Survey Results: Domino's Pizza

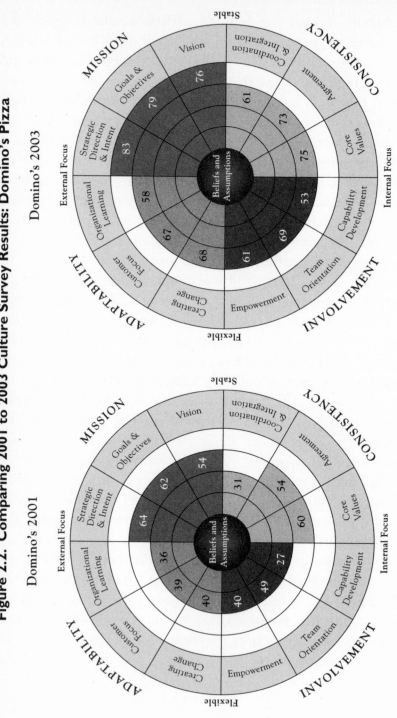

Domino's 2003

Domino's 2001

overall direction of the company. This focus on action helped them to continue their progress.

Following their successful IPO in 2004, Domino's actually accelerated their rate of change. They made some dramatic changes in their people policies that showed a clear impact on the survey results in 2006. These changes were all designed to continue on the path of improving their competitive position by improving the quality of their workforce. They decided that there would be no rehires and no demotions. Although this may sound like a simple HR policy change, consider the impact that it would have. Before this policy was established, many delivery drivers, for example, would work at one store for a while and then, maybe at the end of the college semester, just stop showing up for work; the following year, when they wanted another job, they would show up at another Domino's and get hired back.

At first, store managers objected to the new policy, because it placed some limitations on their ability to hire new drivers. But over time, these changes, along with mandatory drug testing and new store-level software that made it easier to identify "shrinkage" and dishonest store managers, steadily increased the quality of the workforce.

Domino's also focused quite explicitly on getting rid of what they called "coalitions of the unwilling." Those who weren't really "exceptional people on a mission to become the best pizza delivery company in the world" began to stand out against the backdrop of a growing number of people who were on that mission. Attitude and ambition mattered a lot. The leaders took the positive energy and ambition of their people very seriously. They gave a lot, but they also expected a lot in return.

As mentioned earlier, during this time Domino's also made great progress in segmenting the workforce in the entire organization and defining the "pipeline" for each position. From delivery drivers to store managers to vice presidents and future members of the board, each target group understood its pipeline. Which

Figure 2.3. Comparing 2001–2004 Culture Survey Results: Domino's Pizza

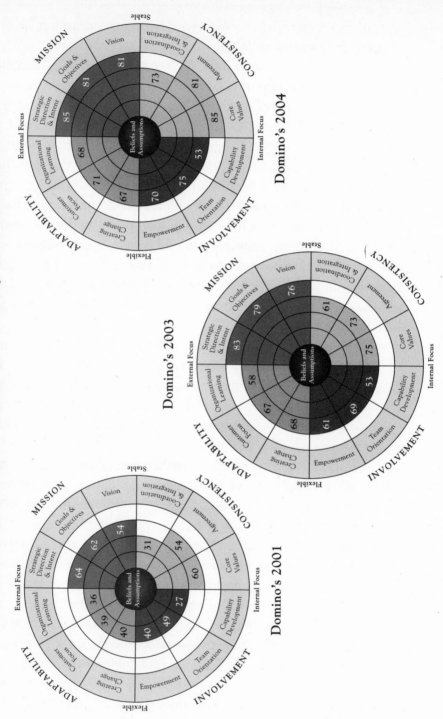

Domino's 2004

Domino's 2003

Domino's 2001

people are at what stage? Who is ready for the next step? What support do they need? Where does the organization need greater depth? The support and energy were very positive, but the organization and its people were held to a higher standard than they had ever seen before.

The Hard Work Pays Off

All of this hard work on improving the organization and the quality of the workforce paid off in the performance of the business. Domino's met most of the goals that they had set at the outset of this transformation, and they made excellent progress against even those goals that they did not meet. Employee turnover was dramatically reduced; profitability, market share, and shareholder returns were increased; and they came close to meeting their goal of being one of the one hundred best companies to work for in America. There are still many challenges in this organization, and they have suffered through several setbacks. But overall, Domino's gives us a great example of how an organization can transform itself by focusing on the way it supports its frontline people. Over the course of five years, Domino's had improved their organization and culture in many ways and created much greater capability on the front line. They received top scores in nearly all areas (see Figure 2.4) and faced the next set of challenges to sustain this high performance culture that they had built.

As mentioned earlier, this transformation also created exceptional value in the marketplace. Domino's became one of Bain Capital's most successful investments, returning 523 percent on their equity investment. On a pizza delivery chain! Mark Nunnelly, managing director at Bain, gave Brandon a lot of credit: "You could put him in the middle of any company and he knew how to focus on key issues. I wish I could clone him."[6]

Figure 2.4. Comparing 2001–2006 Culture Survey Results: Domino's Pizza

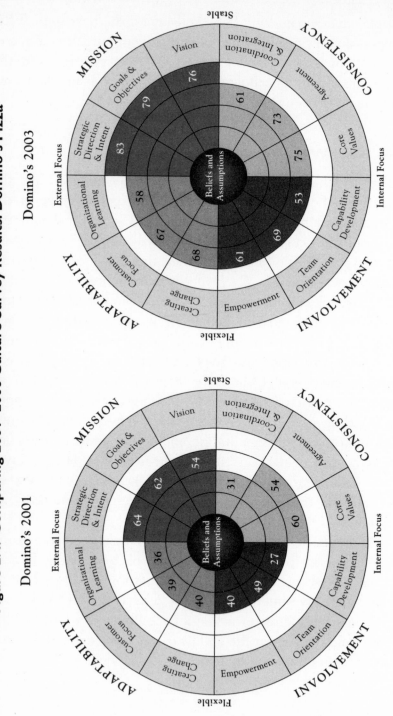

Domino's 2001

Domino's 2003

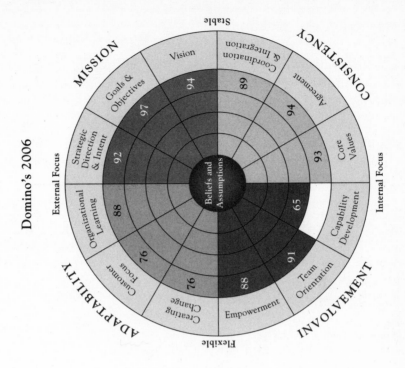

Domino's 2006

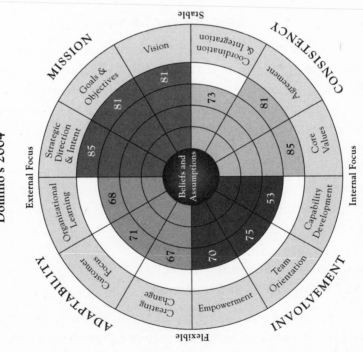

Domino's 2004

Our Role at Domino's

We started doing consulting work using the Culture Survey in the International Division of Domino's for several years before the transformation described in this chapter began. We helped by debriefing the results with the executive team and facilitating an action planning process. We trained a number of Domino's people in interpreting the results and facilitating the action planning process. During the years of the transformation, we met periodically with Domino's to discuss the progress that they were making. But by that time Domino's was very familiar with our approach and drove most of the change process themselves. As we saw the progress that they were making, we also developed an IMD teaching case on the Domino's transformation.

Source: Denison and Lief, 2008.

Lessons for Leaders

There are many lessons about changing the culture of an organization to better support the front line that we can draw from Domino's experience. Like all transformation efforts, it is an interesting mix of changes in mindset and systems, structures, and behaviors, which combines both the magic and the method of a successful change. The survey process helped confirm some of the basic strengths and challenges, and it helped lead Domino's to define a new set of values and behaviors and the policies to support them for the future. Let's look at some of the lessons we can take from their experience.

Lead with a Personal Touch, But Follow Up with Structure

It's hard work to get a culture change process started, but it is even harder work to keep it going. Domino's case is remarkable for how *long* they sustained the transformation process. It is great to talk about "creating a burning platform," but it is more important to understand how to keep the fire going without burning down the house.

The Domino's transformation started largely because of a new CEO with very high expectations, who was positive, inclusive, open, personal, and very visible. Suddenly, everything seemed possible. It was an exciting time. They tell a story about the first time that Brandon went to Mexico City to meet with the Mexican franchisees. When the staff who were organizing the event asked Brandon about his plans for the two-hour meeting, he said that he would just like to make a few opening comments for twenty to thirty minutes and then do Q&A. The staff sat in stunned silence. Domino's had never done a franchise meeting this way before. Typically, the meetings were tightly scripted with a clear agenda with little room for Q&A. After a lot of discussion and extensive nail-biting, they decided to do it Brandon's way. And it was the best meeting that they had ever had with their Mexican franchisees—the message was clear that Domino's had a new energy and flexibility and was fully committed to listening and learning with the franchisees that make up 90 percent of their worldwide sales and to supporting them in the best way that they could.

But unlike many organizations with charismatic leaders, Domino's was also very savvy at creating the structures that sustained that energy and momentum. Creating an enduring system with the structure that exemplifies the new core values lies at the heart of every sustainable culture transformation. For all of the books that have been written about transformational and charismatic leaders whose personal qualities win the day, there is an amazing shortage of books about how successful leaders create structures that leverage the personal characteristics and the values at the core of their transformations. Mindset and systems are often two sides of the same coin. A commitment to improving the quality of the people and listening to the marketplace and the front line is an important value, but the transformation doesn't create much leverage unless leaders create the systems necessary to scale up those values until they reach everyone in the organization—without losing energy and focus.

We Are All in the Service Business

Domino's transformation began when they saw their business through new eyes as a service business that delivered a product, rather than a product business with a lot of delivery people. The difference is simple, but profound: Most of the time, there's not as much difference in the quality of the pizzas that get delivered to your front door as there is in the quality of the people who deliver them. The primary focus of the entire organization needs to be on supporting those who deliver that customer experience.

The fundamental difference in the service business is that the product can never be created independent of the customer experience. So, this means that the front line experience *is* the product, it *is* the strategy, it *is* the organization. There's really no way around it. And the rate of innovation in the customer experience our organizations provide is relentless. The best never rest. But it also requires coordination and consistency! The "frontline" experience for the customer may be a salesperson, a service person, a flight attendant, a driver, a website, an ATM, or someone from tech support. In practice, the front line is the combination of all the ways in which the organization touches the customer. And if the customer experience doesn't add up, guess who takes the fall?

Over most of the twentieth century, production power reigned supreme. If you had the capability to produce the best, the market would follow. Build a better mousetrap, and the world would beat a path to your door. But those days are long gone. Today's power lies with those on the other end of the value chain—those who are closer to the marketplace and the customers. This means that the balance between the value of product knowledge and market knowledge is changing. So is the importance of market knowledge in the mindset and culture of the organization. And this change is happening fast.

Several years into the Domino's transformation, President (and now CEO) Patrick Doyle was planning a tour of some of Domino's stores. He knew that it was very important to be visible on the front line so that his support was clear. But where should he start? There were many choices. His decision was to go directly to individual stores and deliver the message, "We appreciate what you do!" His Appreciation Tour was controversial. Shouldn't the president make an important strategy presentation or give an outline of the goals for this quarter? Or talk about the stock price? Or the competition? Or something really important to the business, like the rising cost of wheat?

No. Instead, in each of the sessions Patrick said a few words about how important the people he was meeting were to Domino's and how much he and the company appreciated them. Then they ate pizza and talked. The president may have gained a few pounds, but he also gained a lot of support from the front line.

What You Keep Is as Important as What You Change

Any way you slice it, Tom Monaghan was a genius at running a pizza shop. From the invention of the "spoodle" by Jeff Goddard, the winner of the 1985 world's fastest pizza maker competition,[7] to the "HeatWave" hot pack for keeping pizzas warm, to the magnetic 3D car-top signs that are now used by many other companies, Domino's boasts an endless string of innovations that have helped perfect the art of running a pizza store. Training standards for new employees require that they be able to make a quality pizza in under one minute. (The fastest pizza makers can make *three* pizzas in one minute!) In fact, during the Domino's transformation, the Investor Relations team was thinking about ways that they could reconnect with the simplicity of their business and reconnect with the front line. Their solution? They decided, as one of their development goals for the year, that all of the members of the Investor Relations team should be able to make a pizza to the Domino's standard in under one minute. It took some of them a while to master this, but they did it.

Monaghan also created an organization structure that required a clear focus on the pizza business. Each franchisee's contract includes Domino's well-known "OBI" provision. A franchisee cannot have any other *outside business interests*. Signing a franchise agreement forces the franchisee to make a commitment to focus exclusively on the Domino's pizza franchise. The company allows some flexibility on this, especially in developing master franchisee relationships when entering new countries. But overall, the new business structure that they've created gives remarkable focus to their efforts. The basic formula is simple: A franchisee with one store has a full-time job and a good income. A franchisee with two stores has two full-time jobs and a very good income. And a franchisee with three stores has three store managers, a full-time job, and a very good income.

Change is good, but successful culture change is not change for change's sake. Developing a clear sense of the policies and practices that need to be preserved and strengthened is an important component of every successful transformation. Domino's makes the point very clearly: Many of the elements of running a successful pizza store have remained unchanged. But the role of the corporate center and the company-owned stores has changed dramatically—these parts of the organization have moved from being the stronghold of the traditionalists to being the core of the innovation process. And one of the most important changes in the role of the corporate center was to work relentlessly to create a system that would dramatically improve the quality and engagement of the people on the front line.

Strategies for Supporting the Front Line: Beyond Domino's

Chris Bartlett and Sumantra Ghoshal positioned the support of the front line as a clear strategic choice for organizations. They argued that many companies are still run with a logic that tries to make the firm immune from human errors.[8] They argue that rather than trying to take the human factor out of the equation and make the organization run like a machine, companies are far better off if they build an environment that harnesses the power of the capabilities of their people.

The themes of participation, involvement, empowerment, and engagement have been with us for a long time. From classic authors such as Douglas McGregor,[9] Rensis Likert,[10] and Ed Lawler[11] to more recent authors such as John Kotter[12] and Jim Collins,[13] many management gurus have argued that the link between the individual and the organization is critical to an organization's success.

Many organizations have focused primarily on the psychological state of their employees. After all, this is the desired result—engaged employees who are committed, satisfied, and productive. But focusing *only* on these desired outcomes misses the most important point: What organizational conditions are the causes for these effects?

You can identify the organizations that have been too influenced by this approach. They often know what they want to achieve for their people, but they are having trouble getting there. The managers talk a lot about "keeping our people happy," but the employees complain that their leaders don't "walk the talk"; the employees then tend to get cynical about attempts to improve things. One manager we met said that he always felt as if he were trying to win the "engaged manager of the year" contest. He saw his organization's engagement efforts as a popularity contest to keep employees happy without really changing very much, rather than a serious attempt to try to improve the organization.

Effective organizations need to focus instead on the environment that they create for their frontline service people. To achieve the desired effect of engaged people on the front line, organizations and their leaders need to be experts in the organizational causes that are necessary to support those frontline people. Organizations that do a good job of supporting their frontline people understand that the psychological state of mind is important, but they focus most of their attention on the working conditions created by their management practices. They are constantly working to improve their culture.

Support Is Strategic: Mickey Mouse Versus the Street Sweepers

Supporting the frontline jobs that have the biggest impact on an organization's customers and their business is probably the most important part of the strategy implementation process. One company that is a perennial leader in this type of thinking is Walt Disney. HR guru John Boudreau shows us how important it is to have a well-conceived strategy for supporting the front line by analyzing the relative importance of the skill levels of Mickey Mouse performers and the sweepers in a Disney theme park.[14]

Mickey Mouse is a very important part of any visitor's experience in a Disney theme park. Mickey gives a warm and friendly greeting to millions of visitors each year. It is a memorable experience and the ideal family photo op. But it doesn't last long. There's little room for improvisation on Mickey's part, and thus, despite the critical importance of Mickey to the overall theme park experience, there is only a small performance difference between the best and the worst Mickeys.

The theme park's street sweepers, however, have a much more pivotal role. As Boudreau notes, the sweepers play a highly important role in customer relations. "People seldom ask Cinderella where to buy a disposable camera, but hundreds a day will ask the street sweeper!"[15] The sweepers need to understand the strategic importance of their role, but this works only if the organization creates a system that recognizes that the sweepers are frontline customer service experts who happen to carry brooms. Selection, training, development, rewards, and future opportunities are all designed to create this context to support their role. Boudreau summarizes this in a graph (Figure 2.5) that shows us why there is more value in improving sweepers' performance than there is

Figure 2.5. Mickey Mouse versus the Street Sweepers

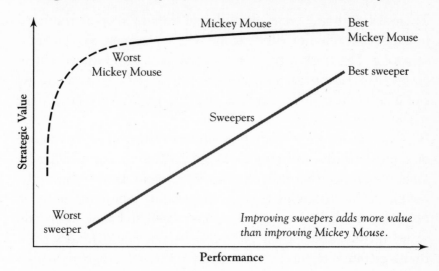

Source: Boudreau and Ramstad, 1961.

in improving Mickey Mouse's performance. It's the context that the organization creates for the street sweepers that makes them highly engaged and highly effective.

Tom Davenport offers additional examples.[16] Harrah's Entertainment studies their organization to the point where they have developed a model that tells them the right number of people to have at the front desk and other key service points throughout the daily cycle. Voilà! They have a dynamic plan that allows their people to react to the changing customer expectations. How happy and engaged can employees be if they never have enough people to cover the front desk? Global food service giant Sysco discovered that the biggest positive impact on customer service came from their experienced delivery associates—those people whose daily deliveries are the lifeblood of every restaurant that they serve. Increased dedication to this pivotal group of front-line people increased their retention rate from 65 percent to 85 percent over six years, leading to major benefits in increased customer satisfaction as well as decreased training and hiring costs.

Know More, Care More, and Contribute More

There are so many great examples of how to support the front line that it's difficult to understand why some organizations get it so wrong. The truth is that this is much easier said than done. A competitive advantage based on people can take years to create. But it also takes years to imitate, and thus gives a great advantage to those who know how to walk the talk.

One of the early leaders in understanding the importance of supporting the front line was Edward E. Lawler III. Lawler argued years ago that the future world of work would require the workforce to "Know more, care more, and contribute more."[17] Frontline workers, he argued, always need to know more and to learn more about their job while they master the new skills that contribute to the business. They also need to care more and have higher emotional involvement in their work and a greater motivation to understand the world from their customers' point of view. Finally, people on the front line need to contribute more. The demand in the marketplace for quality service continues to grow, and the organizations that contribute the most will be the ones that will thrive.

But although Lawler intended these comments for the workforce, it is striking how well they apply to the managers and leaders of organizations, who need to learn the lessons of creating an organization that supports the front line. Their challenge may well be the bigger one: They need to create the set of conditions that allow their frontline people to know more, care more, and contribute more.

We close this chapter with Jon Katzenbach and Jason Santamaria's five guidelines on how leaders can create systems that support the front line.[18]

- *Overinvest at the outset in inculcating core values.* You never get a second chance to make a first impression. Leading companies select people based on the fit with their core values, in anticipation that each new hire will play an important role with respect to the implementation of the strategies of the future. The most important part of each new hire's onboarding experience is not only the skills that they learn, as important as those are, but also about the importance of the core values of the firm.

- *Prepare every person to lead, but especially the frontline supervisors.* Organizations that teach their people that leadership happens only in the executive suite are headed for trouble. The best organizations recognize that leadership has to happen at all levels. To support the front line, it is essential that an organization invest in talented management at the level of the frontline supervisors. Once the chain of command is broken and the front line is disconnected from the rest of the organization, it is hard to put it back together.

- *Distinguish between teams and single-leader work groups.* Supporting the front line means establishing clear accountabilities and decision rights. Fuzzy accountabilities should never be confused with "empowerment." Establishing teams that have collective responsibilities and distinguishing them from individual leaders and supervisors who lead a work group is essential to building a collective sense of responsibility.

- *Attend to the bottom half.* Who gets the most attention? Who has the biggest impact? Every organization can be improved by bringing the bottom half up the middle. You know who they are, where they are, and how they impact the business. And you know how to improve their performance. This is not rocket science. It's much harder! Because it requires not a brilliant conceptual solution, but consistent support and day-to-day commitment .

- *Use discipline to build pride.* If you don't stand for something, you'll fall for anything. A strong set of expectations builds a strong team. A clear standard that everyone must meet means that this is a team or organization that is worth belonging to. Without discipline, it is hard to build a strong sense of pride in belonging.

The role of middle managers is to link the vision of the top to the realities of the marketplace. Want to know how you are doing? Go ask your people on the front line. That's the moment of truth.

3

CREATING STRATEGIC ALIGNMENT

Great strategies make great organizations. But only when they are implemented! A great strategy can focus everyone's attention on the collective purpose, the tactics required, and each individual's role in the process. Great strategies differentiate great organizations from their competition and highlight the unique value that they can create. Finally, great strategies are also built on the complementary capabilities of the organization and its people that no one else can imitate.[1]

But where do these great strategies come from? Examples like Steve Jobs's legendary control over every detail of a new product launch at Apple make it easy to claim that great strategies come from great leaders. But *announcing* a global launch should not be confused with *delivering* a global launch. Apple has mastered both. With each new product announcement, dates are set for the global launch. The product is manufactured and shipped to the stores, arriving the morning of the launch date. Employees are briefed shortly before the product goes on sale, and the crowds gather to see, touch, and buy their new product. The Legend grows.

At Mars, executives still tell the story of a two-day management meeting a few years ago. Day One was in Prague, and Day Two was in Budapest. After lunch on Day One, one of the Mars brothers interrupted the agenda and explained that the team needed to get on the bus because they were going to *drive* to Budapest. Raised eyebrows gave way to wide-eyed stares as the bus stopped at every store along the way to check on the product placement and shelf space given to Snickers, Mars bars, and M&M's. Connecting the big-picture strategy to the action on the ground takes a lot of discipline.

Ram Charan tells the story of DuPont's reaction to the financial crisis in October 2008.[2] Sparked by a conversation with a Japanese customer, CEO Chad Holliday and his top team quickly *formulated* a strategy to conserve cash, so that they could survive in an environment in which capital and credit had disappeared overnight. The more impressive part of the story is that it took only ten days for every employee in the company to have a face-to-face meeting with a manager to identify three things that they could do to conserve cash and reduce costs. It took DuPont only six weeks to create the strategic alignment required to *implement* their plan to conserve cash.

Culture Eats Strategy for Lunch!

A successful business strategy always involves mobilizing people in pursuit of an organizational objective. Organizations must build a strong connection between the positioning of the firm and its products in the marketplace, the systems and structures needed to coordinate the required resources, and the mindset of the individuals who will deliver on the promise. Without careful attention to aligning people, the strategy is just a plan. What happens when a new strategy clashes with an old culture? "Culture eats strategy for lunch!"

This aphorism has been repeated so often that it is hard to determine who said it first. But it always reminds us that *implementing* a business strategy is very different from *formulating* a business strategy.[3] Formulation can occur primarily at the top of organizations, but implementation can work only when *alignment* is achieved across levels, geographies, functions, product lines, and supply chains. After all, managing culture is about managing the balance between external adaptation and internal integration.

It Takes Time to Implement a New Strategy

Rolling out a new strategy takes a lot of time and effort. Consider this example from DeutscheTech, one of Germany's leading technology companies.[4] DeutscheTech has several global business units that serve both consumer and industrial applications. Overall, these businesses generate over $20 billion in annual revenues and employ over fifty thousand workers in over 125 countries.

Culture is important to DeutscheTech, and it goes deep into the roots of a family firm that was founded back in the mid-nineteenth century. At the time that we were working with them, they described one of their core values as preserving that tradition of a family company. The family still has a strong presence in the company, even though their stock has been publicly traded for years. DeutscheTech also recognizes the strength of the bond between the company and its customers and knows the importance of long-term commitment.

Our example comes from DeutscheTech's adhesives business. The company is the global market leader in many of the types of adhesives, sealants, and surface treatments used in manufacturing. Their products help to make cars, appliances, and other manufactured goods quieter, safer, stronger, more comfortable, and more durable. Until 2003, their industrial adhesives and surface treatment technologies had been run as two separate business units. They had separate sales targets, sales forces, management hierarchies, and brands. They used different technologies, and the products were produced in different plants.

But the customers were often the same! Two or three of their salespeople might even be calling on the same client at the same time, competing for their attention, and positioning

DeutscheTech as if it were two small suppliers rather than one large one. In addition, the complementarities between the technologies DeutscheTech uses to prepare metal surfaces for bonding and the adhesives that they use to stick them together were more difficult to realize because they were in two separate business units. So DeutscheTech made the decision to combine these two business units into one.

We tracked DeutscheTech's culture over several years while this strategy was being implemented. Tracking the evolution of their culture over this period of time helped to give us some good insights into the dynamics of the integration process in these two business units. We surveyed all of the levels of management around the world at DeutscheTech for several years using our Organizational Culture Survey. The results presented here describe the perspective of the four levels of management, L1 through L4, in an organization of over four thousand people.

The results presented in Figure 3.1 focus on just one of the twelve indexes, the Vision index. The results show the perceptions of the vision for the business across the four levels of the management hierarchy in the new business unit that combined the adhesives and surface treatments businesses into one organization. There are five items that make up the Vision index as follows:

1. We have a shared vision of what the organization will be like in the future.

2. Leaders have a long-term viewpoint.

3. Short-term thinking often compromises our long-term vision (R).[5]

4. Our vision creates excitement and motivation for our employees.

5. We are able to meet short-term demands without compromising our long-term vision.

The Vision index is the mean score for these five items, which were answered on a five-point Likert scale, with responses

Figure 3.1. The Vision Index

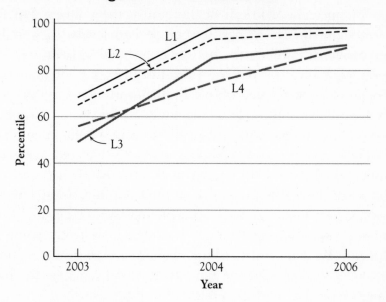

that ranged from strongly disagree to strongly agree. The data in Figure 3.1 are presented as percentile scores, which reflect the percentage of the companies in our benchmark database who scored lower than this target sample.

These results help tell the story of how the leadership team in the adhesives business managed the strategy implementation process. When the management board saw the 2003 results, they realized that there was still a lot of work to do. The plan to integrate the two businesses had been announced throughout the organization, and the structural changes had been made at the top of the business unit. But it was apparent from the results that the overall vision for the business unit still wasn't very clear to the rest of the organization. The business was still production driven, and the products were still produced in different plants. The old mindset of two separate product organizations took time to change. Few of the salespeople could convincingly sell the whole product range, and they needed more cooperation among the different parts of the business to actually deliver for their customers.

As Figure 3.1 shows, the vision score in 2003 was below the 70th percentile for all of the management levels. But the scores were slightly higher at the top two levels, L1 and L2, and somewhat lower for the bottom two levels. Interestingly, the scores were lower for the third level of management than they were for the fourth level, who were the frontline supervisors. We have found that this can be a common situation during a strategic change, as the organization struggles to achieve alignment. The muddle is in the middle. Middle managers have to make the connection between the vision of the top executives and the realities of the marketplace. But on the front line, things haven't changed very much, and some people may still be playing "wait and see," questioning whether the change is really going to happen. The daily reality of the marketplace continues to have a stronger impact than the new strategy and remains the main influence on the mindset of those on the front line.

Figure 3.2 shows the responses across management levels over the same period for one specific item: "There is a long-term purpose and direction." This item is a part of the Strategic Direction and Intent index, which is also part of the Mission trait. These results show an even more dramatic pattern. In 2003, all levels of management were average or below, with L1 and L2 scoring right around the 50th percentile and the two bottom levels scoring 20 points lower. It is normal to see a difference of 5 to 10 percentile points as you move across the levels of an organization, but differences of 30, 40, or even 50 points are usually a strong indication that there is more work to do to achieve alignment. Looking at these survey results across levels helped DeutscheTech to focus on their alignment, but it also forced them to see which parts of the organization needed the most help and attention and where they needed to direct their efforts in order to complete the integration process.

The leadership team in the adhesives business reacted to this situation by focusing more of their attention on the organization. They did more cross-training for their salespeople to ensure

Figure 3.2. "There Is a Long-Term Purpose and Direction"

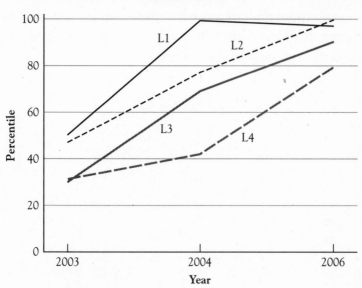

that they could all sell the entire product line. The technical groups cooperated more freely to offer better technical service and support to customers. These changes had a solid impact over the next year, as they showed a significant improvement both in overall vision and in long-term purpose and direction. The third-level managers, in particular, made a big improvement in Vision between 2003 and 2004, as they started to come into alignment with the leadership team in their business unit. But the alignment gap on the long-term purpose and direction item grew wider. At the top, the executives saw the purpose clearly, but the frontline leaders didn't notice that much difference.

Driving this strategic change deep into the organization took still more time. Not until 2006 do we clearly see that all levels of the organization are on board and in alignment. Moving to this stage took an entirely different approach, one that involved two important dimensions: visibility and dialogue. To build alignment, the leadership team took to the road to build their global presence. They explained the new organization, visited customers together with local teams, and most important, spent endless hours in dialogue, until they were sure that everyone in the organization understood what the strategic changes meant for their role. That's what it took to finally achieve alignment between their strategy and their culture.

Our Role at DeutscheTech

We did our first analysis of the DeutscheTech culture as a part of a session on building a high-performance business organization in an IMD executive program in 2000. From this the project expanded dramatically and covered all management levels around the world over a period of four to five years. Annual results of our Organizational Culture Survey were debriefed with the management board and the divisions. We trained the internal organizational development community at DeutscheTech in how to interpret the results and facilitate action planning meetings. Several of us did more extensive consulting work with specific DeutscheTech divisions and locations around the world.

Successful Culture Change Impacts Everyone in the Organization

Our second example of the important role that culture plays in the implementation of strategy comes from the financial services sector. Swiss Re is the world's second-largest reinsurance company, headquartered in Zurich, Switzerland. They were formed in 1863 to reinsure the risks from fires and floods that were being taken by the primary insurers in Switzerland's growing insurance industry. Swiss Re entered the American market in the late nineteenth century and soon paid out most of its capital to cover claims associated with the San Francisco earthquake in 1906. Today they operate in three business areas—property and casualty, life and health, and financial services—reinsuring large risks for primary insurers. Swiss Re's ten thousand employees in twenty-six countries generate revenues of around $30 billion.

Throughout most of the 1990s, Swiss Re competed in a "soft" market with low prices and readily available capital. Insurers had to pursue a top-line growth strategy, even if profitability was lagging. A strong stock market meant that the reinvestment of premium revenues could generate a strong overall return even if the initial investment wasn't very profitable. But by 2000, the business cycle had shifted to a "hard" market, with limited capital, rising prices, and a weak stock market.

The Americas Division was in trouble. Swiss national Andreas Beerli came over from Zurich to replace local management as the new division CEO. He faced a challenging situation: The business was losing money, but the current management team's combination of big-picture vision and decentralized style made it difficult for the organization to react to the crisis. The current leaders were bright, charismatic, and well liked, but they had not built a reputation for establishing a clear direction and getting things done.[6]

Change happened quickly. Andreas rebuilt the management team with new members who were relatively young and very experienced and had a reputation for success. Almost all came from within Swiss Re, but only a few had a prior working relationship with Andreas. In most cases, a few days of working closely together during the first few months of Andreas's tenure as CEO formed the basis for his decision. One observer commented, "In a short period of time, Andreas started making decisions about *who he would trust*. He is a good judge of character and can make decisions very quickly." In twelve to eighteen months he had an entirely new leadership team.

The first change may have been the most important one: Andreas installed the best espresso machine in the building next to his office to encourage everyone to come by and talk. He moved the management board members' offices close together, so that they talked throughout the day, and he created an informal team atmosphere. Slowly a common understanding of the problems and opportunities began to emerge.

The most dramatic transformation took place in the US Direct business, led by French-Canadian Patrick Mailloux. US Direct sold reinsurance products directly to primary insurers, without working through brokers. In one three-day meeting, the new management team designed the new strategy, systems, and behaviors required to move their focus from the top line to the bottom line. But it was their changes to the "operating model" that had the most far-reaching impact. Making a decision about a reinsurance contract typically requires the combination of three separate perspectives: the client representative, the actuary, and the underwriter. The client representative interacts most closely with the client, understands their needs, and usually initiates the proposal for a deal. The actuary assesses the risks and sets a price, and the underwriter writes the contract. During the years when top-line growth was the strategy, the client representative was clearly the top dog. Younger actuaries and underwriters learned to "never say no" to a client representative, who was always motivated to close the deal.

This new operating model created a more equal balance of power in the team, so that any of the three could say "no." This equal power helped ensure that new business contributed to bottom-line performance as well as top-line growth. Their choice of timing to implement this new way of working was bold—they chose to implement this during their annual renewal cycle. Each fall, reinsurance contracts are up for renewal for the following year. It is always a busy time and determines a lot of the company's success for the year. But this year, they were also learning a new model of how to do business. So at the end of each week during the renewal period, they also met together back at headquarters to track their progress and to ensure that their new priorities were in place to deliver on the bottom-line strategy.

US Direct CEO Patrick Mailloux reflected on the factors that were most important to the division's successful transformation:

> We had the freedom to pick the team. We picked very good people, recognized their talents, moved them around, and let the cream rise to the top. We had to tell our message of bottom-line performance to people who had stopped caring. We had to convince them that we meant it and that you can't survive here if you don't care.
>
> I love coming to work here because I get to work with the best. Andreas tells us where we need to go but not how to get there. If you are committed and you perform, then you have autonomy.
>
> We are much more informal now, but much more direct. We have laughter, intellect, frustration. We think that simplicity is sexy. We created a totally different management board within two to three months. My conference table has name plaques for each of the members of the management board. It is a recognition of who is on the team and a reminder that we each need to earn the right to be at the next meeting. I don't expect them to be sitting there converting O_2 to CO_2.

We tracked the Swiss Re culture over this period of time. The changes in the culture scores were dramatic, especially in the US Direct business. Figure 3.3 presents the changes in the overall culture profile, which is one of the most dramatic transformations that we have ever seen. In 2000, all of the scores were in the first quartile, reflecting a human organization that was not up to the task. Things changed slowly at first, but by 2002 they had created a high-performance culture that had transformed the business.

Business performance also changed dramatically over this period of time. Figure 3.4 presents the division's results for this time span, showing dramatic gains over the two years in several aspects of performance. Premium revenues were up by over 50 percent and were accompanied by strong gains in profit results and a marked decrease in expenses.

Figure 3.3. Comparing 2000 to 2002 Culture Survey Results: Swiss Re Americas Division, U.S. Direct Business

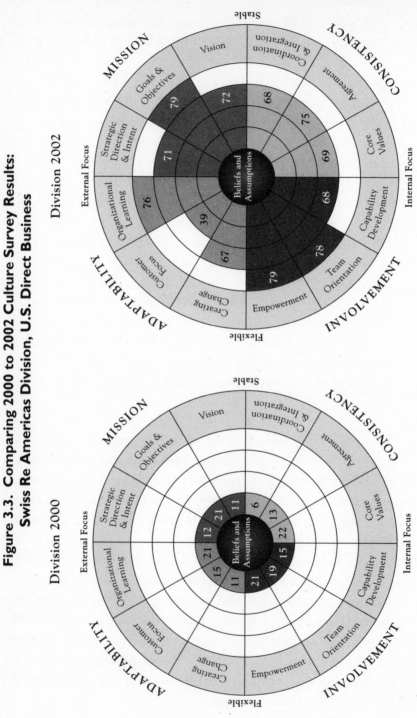

Division 2002

Division 2000

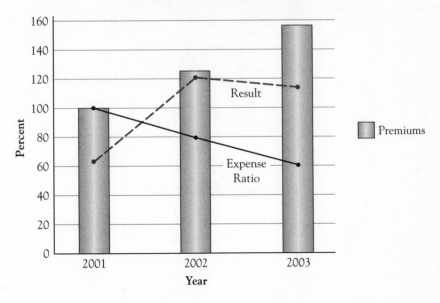

Figure 3.4. Swiss Re Americas Division Operating Performance 2001–2003

Our Role at Swiss Re

Our work at Swiss Re began with an analysis of their organizational culture that was part of an IMD executive program for high-potential leaders. This led to a survey of all Swiss Re employees, which was done for several years. The results were debriefed with the management board, presented at the annual strategy conference, and incorporated into the company's annual planning process.

The results from the Americas Division were handled quite differently. Because the division was going through a transformation, they used the survey results and the action planning process with more depth and regularity. The Americas Division handled all of the feedback and planning processes themselves. And they did it very quickly. One year, we sent them their division results on a Friday morning. On

Friday afternoon, the CEO distributed the results to everyone with an e-mail that said, "Our survey results confirm the progress that we have made this past year. I look forward to working with you to continue our progress this coming year." Discussion and action followed! We also wrote an IMD teaching case on Swiss Re.

Source: Denison, 2004.

Lessons for Leaders

Sometimes there is a big disconnect between those who design a firm's strategy and those who are expected to carry it out. It is very tempting to sit at the top of a successful global corporation and contemplate your strategic options. But it is equally humbling to listen to the office chatter on the front line and realize how little impact your most profound strategic insights have on the day-to-day actions of the people who actually deliver the strategy to your customers. A disconnect makes it difficult to be agile, adaptive, or innovative, and makes it impossible to move fast enough to outflank your competition. But unfortunately, this kind of disconnect is all too common. Believe it or not, one organization that we worked with a few years ago even told us that their new strategy was being communicated only on a "need to know" basis! Creating a new strategy can be fun, but implementing it is hard work. Strategic alignment is the test of how well the organization has done at implementing its strategy.

Several years ago we did a project with 4,500 people in the global purchasing department of a large manufacturing company. We surveyed them all. The results, presented in Figure 3.5, were quite shocking. At the top, the eight-person executive team saw the organization as being very effective. But the buyers, two levels down, saw something dramatically different: They saw an organization with a profile that they called the "donut of doom"!

Figure 3.5. Strategic Alignment in Global Purchasing

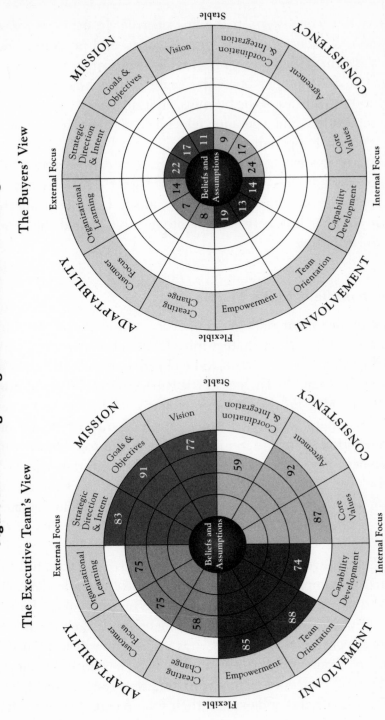

The Executive Team's View

The Buyers' View

All of the scores were in the first quartile. In other words: no mission, no adaptability, no involvement, and no consistency. This extreme type of disconnect is very unusual, but the general dynamic is a familiar one. The cause is detachment from the day-to-day realities of the business, an insulated environment for the top leaders, and a genuine reluctance on their part to engage their people in open discussion.

Many lessons about strategic alignment can be drawn from the two case studies presented in this chapter. These lessons can be applied in any organization that wants to build a culture that creates a tight link between boardroom strategy and the action on the front line.

The Muddle Is in the Middle

Lack of alignment seldom occurs because top executives don't want to translate their strategy into action or because their people on the front line don't want to be effective in their roles. As we saw in the DeutscheTech case, the battleground is almost always in the middle. So the first step is always to understand where the disconnect actually occurs. Strategic alignment is built one conversation at a time. So it may start at the top, but creating alignment across the entire organization means that people at each level and location need to understand the strategy and their role in its implementation. The role of middle managers is to connect the vision of the top leaders to the reality of the marketplace.[7]

The chain of command is only as strong as its weakest link. To manage the implementation of a strategy, new or old, leaders need to find that weakest link and help them out. For all of the talk about "taking out levels of management" and "creating flatter, more responsive organizations," it is amazing how little discussion there is about finding those in the middle who don't clearly understand their role in implementing the strategy, and taking the time to discuss and explain their role. As often as not, when leaders take the initiative to have this discussion—"managing by walking around," as Tom Peters called it—they learn a lot about the logic of their organization and the gaps between the strategy, the marketplace, and the capabilities of the firm. In addition, the visibility and accessibility of the leaders builds trust and commitment when they show an interest in how the firm's strategy looks to their people across the levels of their organization.

Simplicity Is Sexy

I never thought that the reinsurance business could be sexy until I heard Swiss Re executive Patrick Mailloux say this. His message was clear: When the purpose is compelling, the goals are well understood, and the roles are well defined, it creates a focus that builds energy. The shared sense of purpose frees people up, even as they work intensely together as a team to get the job done. Simplicity requires that everyone "gets it." The role of understanding cannot be overestimated. If people are still confused, the organization can't have a sense of simplicity. And that's not very sexy!

An organization's culture also plays an important role in resolving ambiguity and helping people sort out unfamiliar situations. Well-developed organizational cultures give a lot of redundant signals about the right and wrong ways to do things. All of the signs point in the same direction. The underlying assumptions and core logic of the firm provides a common point of reference that helps us find a simple response to a complex situation.

Deciding Who to Trust

One of the best lessons about leading change came from Andreas Beerli, CEO of Swiss Re's Americas Division in our case study. He didn't say it himself, but the point came through loud and clear from several executives on his new management team, as they talked about the way Andreas decided who he was going to trust with the key roles on his management team.

They noted that Andreas typically made up his mind about who he was going to trust for key roles in a relatively short period of time—usually within several months. He didn't just bring in former colleagues or pick from established relationships, but instead made his decisions based on intensive interactions over relatively short periods of time. One of his executives gave an example of spending two or three days working together with Andreas a couple of different times, over a period of six weeks while they were working on the new strategy. After that, Andreas asked him to join the management team.

The message from all of these stories was clear: You can't wait forever to decide whom you are going to trust. And the longer that you wait to choose, the more likely people are to conclude that you aren't going to trust anyone. Once this decision is made, the new team starts to come together. Andreas usually picked younger people who had a record of high achievement, great knowledge of the business, and a high level of energy. But trust came first. Trust allows you to move fast.[8]

A Successful Transformation Has an Impact on Everyone

Successful transformations require deep involvement. Another important lesson from the Swiss Re case emerges from when they redefined their "operating model." To move from a top-line strategy to a bottom-line strategy, they needed to make decisions about a new business opportunity with a three-person team at the table: a client representative, an actuary, and an underwriter. This was a big departure from the days of the top-line strategy, when the client representatives held the most power. This power shift and new way of working together influenced thousands of decisions—and hundreds of people, as they learned a new way to work together to breathe life into the new strategy.

This case is also a great example of how important it is to find the pulse of the organization when you are trying to create a change. Swiss Re implemented this change in the middle of the busiest period of the year: the renewal season in the autumn, when all of their contracts were updated and renewed for the coming year. They certainly would have had more time to put the new operating model in place if they had waited until after the first of the year. But timing is everything. If the changes are not implemented when they really count, then the opportunity has been lost until the next cycle comes around. When you are trying to change an organization, you must understand the dynamics of your organization's business cycle. What timing gives you the greatest leverage with which to drive the change process? In the fashion business, for example, designers always create new styles two or three seasons ahead of the time when they will actually be sold. Trying to intervene when the new products are already on the way to the stores would be pointless. So it is very important to "find the pulse" and use that cycle to build momentum for the transformation.

Creating Strategic Alignment: Beyond DeutscheTech and Swiss Re

Strategic alignment is always achieved by creating a clear cycle that connects strategy formulation and strategy implementation. The strategies that are formulated need to reflect the business realities on the ground. This means that the experience of all levels of an organization is critically important to formulating a new strategy. When formulation is done only at the top, there is an increased likelihood that the organization will choose a strategy that it cannot really implement. The top, the middle, and the bottom all need to collaborate in order to bring together knowledge from both inside and outside the organization. In some firms and industries the best vantage point for understanding the competition is at the top, where the leaders can see the latest developments in the marketplace. But in other firms the best knowledge of the competition is on the front line, where the battle is fought every day. In other firms, the best understanding of the competition is in the design studio or the R&D labs, where relentless product improvements are constantly created. The alignment of all of these forces is what characterizes the most successful strategies.

When it comes to implementation, the link between the top, the middle, and the bottom becomes even more important. The implementation process is the only way to execute the strategy—and the only way to test the strategy. After all, you can't really judge the success of a new strategy until you have actually tried it. So up and down the line there are two goals that must be pursued in parallel: execution and learning. "Just do what I say" might sometimes be good advice for execution, but it is most often poor advice for learning.

The Cycle of Strategy Formulation and Implementation

One of the most useful ways to look at the cycle of strategy formulation and implementation is the one provided by balanced scorecard gurus Robert Kaplan and David Norton. An overview of their model is presented in Figure 3.6.[9]

Kaplan and Norton point out that the process usually starts at the top, with mission, vision, and values. Translating this plan into action requires a set of measures, targets, and strategic initiatives for all of the different parts of the organization. Next comes planning and implementing this at an operational level. But after this stage the focus turns to monitoring and learning and then to testing and adapting. This learning process is a key part of developing the strategy for the next cycle. Then the process starts all over again.[10] Organizations that do this well can create "a performance-directed culture ... one in which everyone is actively aligned with the organization's mission; transparency and accountability are the norm, new insights are acted on in unison, and conflicts are resolved positively and effectively."[11]

Figure 3.6. Balancing Strategy Formulation and Implementation

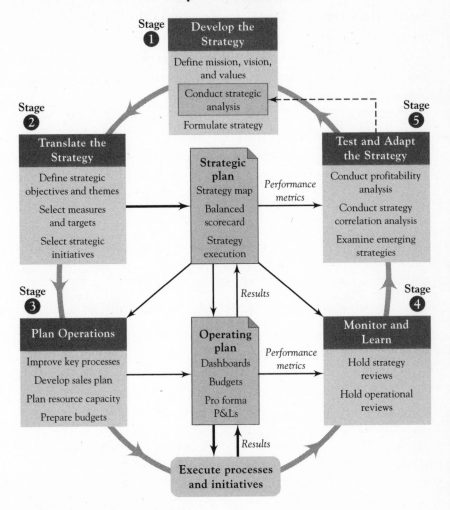

Source: Kaplan and Norton, 2008.

Mobilizing Mindset

The link between the mindset of the people and the logic of the system that they create is always at the heart of the alignment process. The mindset and the system are two sides of the same coin. Sometimes we can change our mindset by immersing ourselves in a new system. But other times, "successful change only comes when we view the world with new eyes."[12] The survey process in each of these organizations helped them see that the mindset and systems that they had created in the past were no longer suited to their current challenges. That insight built a lot of energy and ambition and drove them to innovate together and to plan a future that would be different from the past.

4

CREATING ONE CULTURE OUT OF MANY

One Shell. One EMC. One Metso. One Merck. One Deloitte. One IBM. Nearly all of the companies that we work with today are trying hard to integrate the disparate parts of their far-flung global empires into one coherent whole. "Enterprise thinking" refers to the mindset that allows people to act on behalf of the organization as a whole, rather than representing just one part of it. Even when companies grow organically, it is often harder than it looks. Consider this story: after a round of golf, legendary GE CEO Jack Welch allegedly asked equally legendary Canon CEO Fujio Mitarai if it was possible to get one global price and service agreement for Canon copiers for GE worldwide. Mitarai-san confirmed that they could do it. But when Mitarai went back to his organization, he heard a different story. Because of the structure of Canon's highly successful regional sales companies in the United States and Europe, it took a lot of extra work to negotiate one global price and one service agreement. Global integration is a big challenge.[1]

But when companies grow through acquisition, the challenge is even greater. When Hewlett-Packard acquired IT solutions provider EDS, the combination was irresistible. H-P sold products. EDS sold services. The merger offered them both a way to compete more directly with the giant in their industry, IBM Global Services. But achieving the high-quality integration necessary to fulfill the promise takes a lot of time and effort. When Canon acquired the Dutch printing and solutions company Océ in 2009, the stakes were even higher. Not only did they need to integrate products and solutions such as HP and EDS, but they also needed to do so across national boundaries. Canon was Japanese, Océ was Dutch, and the Americas were a big competitive market, where the integration needed to go smoothly in order to make the acquisition a success.

E Pluribus Unum

Mergers pose the greatest integration challenges when multiple aspects of the corporate identities involved are stacked up against one another. Cross-border mergers, when integration spans national borders, can be very difficult.[2] But mergers that span business sectors, like HP-EDS, and require the integration of products and services also present a lot of complications. What about the customers? Daimler-Chrysler failed for many reasons, but the differences between the automotive industry's premium segment and the mass-market segment certainly added to the challenge. When mergers throw in a new combination of technologies, new ownership and governance structures, and a different leadership style and history, then the Holy Grail of synergy becomes harder and harder to attain. In the words of one M&A veteran: "Buying is fun; merging is hell."[3]

Difficulty in aligning these deep-rooted cultural differences is one of the main reasons that many mergers are unable to deliver on their promise.[4] Corporate cultures are built up of all of the interlocking habits and routines that make up an organization's formula for success. But evolving beyond their past success requires an organization to rethink the past and unlearn those practices and principles that need to stay in the past and to reinvent the new organization that will lead them into the future. Their future success depends on the quality of this process.

This chapter examines these issues by focusing on the efforts of the Scandinavian financial services firm Polar Bank as they struggled to integrate three strong cultures into one company.[5] For several years after the initial acquisition there was little progress. But then a new CEO, Katarina Hansen, started to focus on the whole company—rather than the individual banks—and tried to move the organization from the point of talking about integration to the point of doing something about it.

History Has Its Own Logic

Polar Bank grew out of the 1996 merger between the Norwegian retail bank Fylkesbanken and Sweden's Ländesbanken, a leader in pubic financing. Fylkesbanken also held a controlling interest in Denmark's oldest private bank, the International Bank of Denmark (IBD), with Ländesbanken as a minority partner. IBD was focused on asset management. So, three different corporate entities, three different countries, three different traditions, and three different sectors of the financial services industry. The vision for this combination was compelling: They wanted to create the leading Scandinavian full-service bank with strengths in retail, public financing, and asset management.

But for several years after the merger, these three different banks continued to operate quite independently; each bank focused on its home country. The companies had very different organizational cultures. Fylkesbanken's strength was in their local retail presence throughout Norway. Basically they operated as a national federation of small-town retail bankers. Ländesbanken also had a strong local presence throughout their home country of Sweden, but their strength was in serving the public financing needs of Swedish municipalities, a very different segment of financial services. In addition, several smaller organizations that were acquired since the 1996 merger—such as the Norwegian insurance company that they bought in 2002 or the Finnish retail bank that they had acquired in 2004—had also remained independent. Each bank's executives were totally focused on their own local performance and were not very concerned about Polar Bank as a whole. After all, why should asset managers in one country be concerned about how retail bankers in another country did their jobs?

Tracking the Transformation

When Katarina Hansen was promoted to CEO of Polar Bank in January 2005, she quickly concluded that the future of Polar Bank was limited as long as the bank remained a collection of unintegrated acquisitions. She felt that they would be vulnerable to acquisition and would never achieve a dominant position in the Scandinavian market if they weren't well integrated. Hansen had been associated with the bank since the 1996 merger, first as their outside counsel, then as a board member, and for the prior four years as the head of their office of general counsel. Her affiliation with the corporate center rather than one of the individual banks was viewed as an important strength for her new role as CEO. But the results from our Culture Survey showed that she had her work cut out for her.

The survey results showed that Polar Bank's strategy and vision were not clear (see Figure 4.1). These also showed that they lacked coordination and integration across business lines and borders. They had not built one team and hadn't created a consensus to move toward one overarching culture. Nor were they very focused on customer satisfaction. But despite this lack of attention to the creation of a single culture, Polar Bank still showed many signs of being a good employer, with notable strengths in capability development and in the empowerment of their people in the corporate center as well as in each of the banks. The survey results from the three banks had a lot

To Hansen, these survey results signaled that it was time to start addressing the problems and recognizing that Polar Bank was still made up of three different cultures. She totally agreed with the previous CEO's vision that the bank should operate as one company. But even though the previous CEO had talked a lot about operating as one company since the 1996 merger, few changes had actually occurred. Polar Bank's structures and processes remained mostly unchanged, and the top team was not truly engaged in the integration process. They met every two weeks, but usually just went back home and ran the banks the same way that they always had. Hansen knew she had to transform the bank quickly if her vision was to become a reality. Based on the survey results, she decided to focus on the strategy process, the governance structure, and the development of their top leaders.

Developing One Strategy

Trying to lead one organization with three separate strategies hadn't worked very well. But developing one strategy would require the executives and managers to build a much greater understanding of each other's businesses and strategies. To start this process, Hansen organized a series of strategy workshops with managers from all levels of the three banks to join in an open discussion on the strategy of each business unit. Integrating three banks with three different strategies required a big investment of time and effort. Only if they understood the other banks' current strategies could they understand what they could accomplish if they worked together.

The managers generally agreed with the basic approach of building the bank around business lines that spanned national boundaries. But there was no consensus on how to do this. To succeed, Hansen realized, she would need deep involvement from many levels of the organization and therefore created a combined cross-business and bottom-up approach to strategy development. This meant that the senior managers from the retail bank in Norway needed to understand and buy into the strategy for the public finance bank in Sweden and vice versa. These multidepartmental strategy discussions sent a strong signal to all of the groups that Hansen was serious about developing one overarching strategy and culture for Polar Bank. In addition to senior managers, she also involved a large group of high potentials in the strategy process. By June 2005, this process had helped to clarify and communicate the strategic vision: Polar Bank clearly aspired to be the major player in retail banking in Scandinavia and to be a European leader in public finance and asset management.

Communicating One Message

Communicating her message about the strategic vision to all stakeholders was also important. Hansen's message was that better integration was essential to Polar Bank remaining independent. Without better cross-border and cross-business integration, Polar Bank was likely to be acquired by a competitor as part of the ongoing industry consolidation in Europe. Hansen's message was that the banks that were the best at integrating their acquisitions would be the most likely to survive the consolidation of the industry.

She started with her top team. She argued that they needed to get passionate about the integration, even though passion was not always a top priority among her bankers. She walked a fine line, stressing that Polar Bank was "not desperate to find a partner before it is too late," but that they had to be stronger if they were going to be able to continue operating as a stand-alone company.

This message had to be communicated both internally and externally. Hansen organized meetings in the three different entities at the same time as a June 2005 meeting with financial analysts to discuss Polar Bank's new strategy. While she was in Norway with the analysts, members of the group management board were present at the Swedish and Danish locations and delivered the same presentation. This new approach to communication was a clear break with the past, when all communication was focused on the issues facing the individual banks. Shortly after the announcement of the strategy, Polar Bank also acquired a Finnish retail bank. This showed both the employees and other stakeholders that Polar Bank was serious about its strategy and that it would allocate its resources in ways to support their ambitions.

Creating One Corporate Center

Since the 1996 merger, the corporate headquarters of Polar Bank had acted more like a holding company than a strong corporate center—only corporate finance had any real influence. The corporate center did not have an overall strategic plan or a set of staff departments such as human resources, information technology, or back-office operations. As in a holding company, each bank was focused on maximizing its own profits rather than creating synergies and maximizing the profits of the Polar Bank group as a whole. In order to move forward, they created stronger human resources, finance, marketing, and branding in the corporate center. They also made an effort to spread best practices across the different banks. Finally, Polar Bank ensured that the best people had opportunities throughout the organization rather than in the bank in which they were based.

Creating One Board

Hansen took another step forward by restructuring the management boards of each of the three entities. Each bank's board now included the CEO of all three banks, Hansen, and three other members of the group management board. This new arrangement reinforced the idea that each bank's CEO had to operate with a group mindset. More than any other single step, this move gave a strong and decisive signal that Hansen was serious about creating a bank that operated as a single entity and not as three separate ones.

Creating One Team

Hansen also realized that she must have people who believed passionately in the vision. She worked to ensure that the right people were in the right positions. One key human resource executive, for example, did not openly reject Hansen's approaches, but did give a lot of passive resistance. Some key strategies—such as 360-degree feedback and coaching for top management, and using the corporate university to develop executives from all three banks and the corporate center—received only lukewarm support from this executive. People quickly noticed, and it made them wonder how serious Hansen was about the making the changes. So she asked him and several other capable but slow-moving executives to leave.

Creating One Leadership Development Process

Hansen knew that she had to align all of Polar Bank's systems and structures to support her efforts to change the culture. The Polar Bank corporate university developed a leadership program in which senior executives from all of the banks worked on their leadership skills. Teams of managers focused on five key leadership dimensions: customer orientation, vision, innovation, people management, and cross-boundary collaboration. Each team had a board member sponsor, and six weeks after the program, they presented the management board with their ideas, some of which they adopted on the spot.

Hansen and the management board also led the way in the widespread use of 360-degree feedback and coaching. Actions speak louder than words. Since then, over four hundred top leaders have taken part in this feedback and coaching process. The corporate university created a program to rotate young, high-potential managers around the three banks for six-month assignments. This was another instrumental step in breaking down Polar Bank's silo mentality, promoting managers' understanding of its different subcultures, and creating a pool of mobile international managers. Polar Bank also implemented talent reviews to help identify and manage talent across boundaries.

Tracking the Transformation

The changes that Hansen and her team had put into place slowly started to have an effect. In September 2006, about eighteen months after she took over as CEO, she decided to repeat Polar Bank's Culture Survey to assess the progress that they had made. As is the case for many organizations, she saw major improvements in the areas where they had put the most attention. All elements of mission improved dramatically: Strategy and vision increased by over fifty points each, and the clarity of goals and objectives also grew dramatically. All of the work that they had done to clarify the direction of the bank for the future was starting to sink in. These results are presented in Figure 4.3.

Polar Bank's second survey also showed substantial progress in two other areas. The level of teamwork had improved by more than thirty points. Their progress in organizational learning, where they had improved by fifty points, was mostly in the area of risk and innovation, again showing that the areas they had given the most attention showed the biggest improvement.

The Polar Bank scores also showed that they remained strong in empowerment and capability development, confirming that they had never strayed far from their strengths as a good employer even while they were carrying out all of these changes.

Perhaps the most frustrating part of these results, however, was what had not improved. Customer focus remained at a low level, showing little or no improvement. In addition, nearly all of the measures of consistency had stayed right where they were in the first survey. Perhaps the groundwork had been laid for a

Figure 4.3. Comparing 2004 to 2006 Culture Survey: Polar Bank

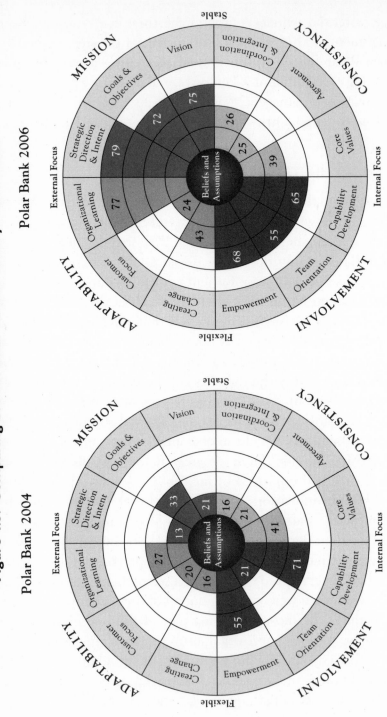

Polar Bank 2006

Polar Bank 2004

common infrastructure and set of values, but they were still a long way from creating one common operating system.

Lessons for Leaders

Leaders must recognize the strong subcultures in their organizations. They arise from influences both from within the organization and from the outside. In some organizations—like a holding company, a conglomerate, or another highly decentralized organization—this level of fragmentation can be desirable. Nonetheless, most organizations try hard to create a common culture and integrate the pieces into a compelling whole. Polar Bank made a clear strategic choice to forgo the option of continuing to operate as three separate banks and to become a full-service bank with cross-border business units.

But changing culture is hard work, and it needs to take place at a very practical level. Hansen could never have made the progress that she did by simply stating: "Polar Bank will have one overarching culture" and then hoping that it would happen. She learned that you need to take strong, concrete actions if you want culturally distinct businesses to behave in the best interests of the overall company.

Create a Common Governance Structure

One of the best lessons from Polar Bank comes from their decision to create one common board of directors to govern all three banks. Having the same identical board for all three banks created a common governance structure and significantly reduced the internal power struggles. Concern about the power differences among the banks became secondary to their shared interest in having each of the three banks operating successfully and all moving toward a future in which they could work together to exploit their complementarity and achieve the new dynamic capabilities required to fulfill their strategic mission.

Few companies that we know of have used this approach to resolving governance issues in the same way that Polar Bank has. A more common practice is for some exchange of board members and roles between companies. For example, in the pharmaceutical industry, when DSM acquired Roche Vitamins in 2002, a member of the DSM executive board became the chairman of the newly acquired company, and DSM also appointed one of their own executives as the new CEO of the vitamin business.

Engage the Leaders in Building a Common Strategy

When striving to achieve one overall company culture, different business units have to understand each other's strategies. Another good lesson from Polar Bank's experience was the impact of their efforts to involve senior executives and high-potential managers of each of the three banks in the strategy development for all of the banks. The time that the leaders spent together understanding each other's strategies also helped them understand each other's operations, markets, products, people, and culture, as well as their strengths and weaknesses. It served as a general mechanism by which the three banks could learn about each other's businesses as well as the primary purpose of crafting a common strategy.

Although we have not seen cross-business strategy development to this same extent in other companies, we have seen some other interesting examples. In one European pharmaceutical company, for example, they required very broad involvement in the continued development of the corporate strategy. Every five years they go through a process known as the corporate strategy dialogue (CSD). Hundreds of managers, from all levels, are involved in the process. In addition, when the business units translate the corporate strategy into a strategy for their own business unit, they typically ask executives from some of the other business units to conduct a critical review of their plans.

Build Cross-Business Capability

Polar Bank also built cross-business capability by establishing a system of job rotation. The career paths of the high-potential leaders in all three banks now would require spending several years in at least one of the other banks. This was often quite unpopular, because it required successful people to move outside of their home country and to take some new risks. But it was also extremely helpful in identifying those individuals who were truly committed to the cross-border mission and strategy.

However, talking about job rotation and actually doing it are two different things. One other company that we worked with also instituted a system of "job rotation." It all sounded good in principle; in practice, though, all of the rotation went one way. Senior managers from the acquiring company were "rotated" to important positions in the acquired company. But the people whose jobs they were rotated into soon found out that they were being "rotated" out of the company. It did not take people long to see that this was all about the victors claiming the spoils, and the acquiring company imposing its culture on the acquisition, rather than working on the creation of a best-of-both culture by moving people both ways.

Make Quick Decisions About Managers Who Aren't Aligned

Katarina Hansen was also quite deliberate in her decisions about those executives who weren't aligned with the transformation she was trying to achieve at Polar Bank. She was patient, and she gave managers ample opportunity to show their energy and alignment. She definitely didn't "shoot from the hip." But when it was clear to her that some of her team members were not supportive of the strategy and the culture changes that were required, she took quick action. Getting the team right from the beginning is always the first step in the integration process.[6]

Creating One Culture Out of Many: Beyond Polar Bank

We once worked with a UK-based beer company that had grown significantly through a decade of acquisitions. Repeated attempts to integrate the acquisitions into one organization proved difficult and never created nearly as much excitement and energy among the top leaders as the next acquisition target. They saw the discussion of "creating one culture" as a fluffy discourse about values and purpose, but at the same time they were constantly frustrated with their repeated failure to establish a common framework so that they could implement basic business decisions—like rationalizing production and establishing a common branding and distribution system across their far-flung empire.

Still, some of their people kept talking about their values and their culture. One evening the EVP for HR took me aside and talked for a few minutes about those who were suggesting that the leadership team should spend more time talking about their own core values and paying more attention to the creation of a common culture. He asked me if I would be able to meet with their management team sometime soon to discuss this issue with them and help them decide their next steps.

"What do you want to achieve?" I asked him.

He looked at me, raised one eyebrow, and said, "We need to make sure nothing happens!"

I took a long walk back to the hotel that evening.

A few years later, they received a good offer from one of their competitors to buy this whole collection of unintegrated acquisitions. It was a great opportunity to sell both the problems and the possibilities on down the line. They took the offer. Live by the sword, die by the sword. Integrating acquisitions is a lot of work!

Creating an Integration Plan

The classic way to frame this discussion, after many years, is still the Mirvis and Marks model, presented in Figure 4.4. In their

Figure 4.4. Different Types of Mergers

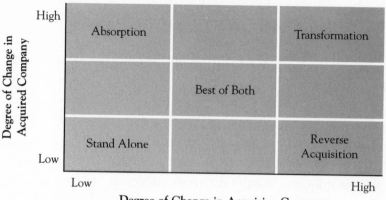

Source: Mirvis and Marks, 1991.

2010 book, *Joining Forces: Making One Plus One Equal Three in Mergers, Acquisitions, and Alliances,*[7] they compare the degree of change required in the acquired company with the degree of change in the acquiring company. From this they describe five different types of mergers.

- "Stand-alone" mergers, which require little change in either company
- "Absorption" mergers, in which the acquired company must change dramatically so that it can be absorbed by the acquiring company
- "Reverse acquisition" mergers, in which the acquiring firm must change dramatically to take on many of the characteristics of the acquired firm
- "Transformational" mergers, which require dramatic changes from both organizations
- "Best of both" mergers is a middle ground requiring a moderate level of change in both organizations

Understanding these categories always serves to clarify the power dynamics and complexities that are associated with any merger. But confusion over which category best fits the situation is always a sign of trouble.

The second step in the Mirvis and Marks framework addresses the question of how much integration is needed. Where? When? Why? In what order? Should the components of the new organization just be separate parts of a common holding company? Or should they be fully merged and consolidated? There are many attractive midpoints along the way. Different business units and functions may also require different strategies, and some of these targets of integration may evolve from one category to the other over a period of several years. A detailed integration plan is the best resource to create to guide the integration process (see Figure 4.5).

Figure 4.5. How Much Integration?

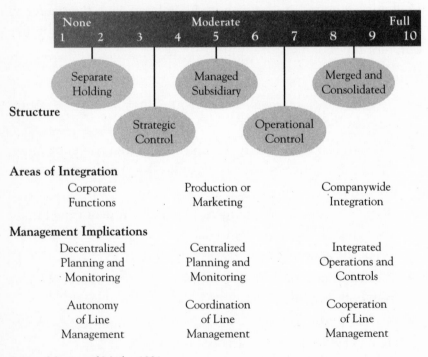

Source: Mirvis and Marks, 1991.

It is also important to recognize that the similarities and differences between two corporate cultures can be a source of both strength and challenge. Organizations usually look for similarities first and tend to see those as strengths. Our favorite example of this comes from IBM Consulting's acquisition of PricewaterhouseCoopers Consulting.[8] As the integration team completed their due diligence on the two companies, they noted some remarkable similarities in the organization structures, market strategies, and company values. Then, when the combined executive leadership team was able to rapidly agree on their new operating principles, it seemed to some of the leaders that the two organizations were really like "twins separated at birth!" In the beginning of the "hunt" it is easy to underestimate the complexities of the integration process.

But it is also important to see that the complementarities between very different cultures, if managed well, can be a tremendous source of strength. Large, stable technology companies often acquire small, dynamic start-ups to drive their innovation and growth. When the process is managed correctly, the combined organization is able to achieve leverage on their innovative ideas in a way that the start-up alone never could. When pharmaceutical companies make R&D acquisitions, they may pay a high price, but they may be able to achieve greater return on that investment than they can from the same investment in their own R&D labs.

Cultural incompatibility is, on occasion, a good reason for avoiding an acquisition target altogether. But more often, if an organization pays careful attention to the cultural complexities of the integration process, and combines that with a thoughtful integration plan that maintains the right balance between patience and urgency, it can beat the odds and manage its way to a successful outcome.

5

EXPORTING CULTURE CHANGE

Every global organization faces the same challenge. It doesn't matter whether they are American, Dutch, Swiss, Chinese, German, French, Japanese, Brazilian, or Indian: their organization started in one place and grew successfully from there. The core logic and the established culture of the firm reflect those origins. As their organization has thrived, it has grown far beyond their initial origins and aspirations. But in the process, they start to bump up against a basic dilemma: How do you export the spirit, the essence, and the principles that form the foundation of a successful organization to a new context without falling victim to the folly of imposing home country habits in a new setting where those habits don't fit very well?

Examples are everywhere. How do you sell hamburgers in India? Yes, management consultants are fond of saying that "sacred cows make the best burgers," but that doesn't help McDonald's create a product strategy for Hindu customers.[1] When Domino's Pizza first entered Germany, they tried to stick to the formula that had worked for them in the States. But they quickly found out that most German men would not take their families out for pizza if they couldn't sit down at a table and have a beer. So they had to change their plans to adapt to the local habits. In Chapter One, we talked about the fact that IKEA's flatpack strategy made it nearly impossible for them to really prosper in the commercial furniture market. However, they have successfully introduced lingonberries as an icon of Swedish style in many different countries. Building a successful global corporation always means successfully importing and exporting elements of an organizational culture across national boundaries.

When Japanese companies first began building cars in the United States in the 1980s, they tried, with mixed success, to introduce Japanese work practices into their American factories. One practice that didn't transfer very well was the Japanese habit of workers doing calisthenics together before starting work in the morning. I never understood why this practice worked so well with Japanese workers until our oldest child Roland went to fifth grade in a Japanese public school. Every morning, even in the winter, the students would line up in the playground at the beginning of the day. Their teachers would call roll, make announcements, and talk about the plans for the day. While they talked, the children shivered, but did not dare to complain. When the teacher stopped talking, the exercises would begin! Slowly, the day would come alive, as the children started to warm up together.

So for a Japanese worker, morning calisthenics has a lot of meaning with deep roots in their national culture. But the same practice had very little meaning for the American workers, so it didn't achieve the intended purpose. These stories are good reminders for all of us that meaning makes sense only in context. When we change context, we always need to make sure we *connect*.

Can Culture Change Be Exported?

A successful transformation of any one part of an organization is a major achievement. But translating those changes to another part of the organization is a far bigger challenge. Achieving uniform change on a global scale is the biggest challenge of all. It is difficult because organizations seldom change at the same pace throughout the world. Many firms make the mistake of assuming that they can roll out programmatic change on a global basis. In our experience, it is quite different. All change is local, and then multilocal, long before it becomes global. Learning from local best practice, so that the most important lessons are transmitted to the entire firm, is the hardest part of the change process. The seeds of the future always exist in the present, where they are waiting to be discovered and leveraged on a global scale.

This perspective implies that transforming a global organization requires successful change in one part of the organization to be "exported" to other parts of the firm and then integrated into the local context. Is that really possible? What does it take to make this process successful? Let's have a look at one example of a successful transformation in the United States that was then "exported" to Europe.

Transformation and Turnaround

In 1998, GT Automotive acquired S&H Fabrication and formed the HVAC Division (heating, ventilation, and air conditioning) to serve the automotive market.[2] GT was a private company that originated in 1919 in Birmingham, England, as Tube Investments Ltd. From the start, GT was an industrial company specializing in products that carried fluids through tubing, such as braking systems, fuel systems, and HVAC systems. Through the decades, the company grew organically and through acquisitions (the company is now owned by a private equity firm). By 2009, they operated over a hundred facilities in twenty-seven nations with sixteen thousand employees on six continents. Of around $3 billion in annual sales, Europe generated 50 percent; North America, 35 percent; and the remainder came from Asia and South America. GT is a supplier to every major auto manufacturing company, and General Motors is their largest customer.

In 2002, Tim Kuppler became general manager of GT's North American HVAC Division. Kuppler was a veteran employee of GT, having joined the company in 1992. His experience in the company included ten years in quality assurance, followed by a stint in fuel systems. He inherited the leadership role in an organization that had gone through a lot of transition and was the ninth leader to take charge of the organization within the last five years!

Since the S&H acquisition, all administration has been centralized around the North American headquarters near Detroit. Many long-term employees felt that the innovative and entrepreneurial culture of S&H had been replaced with the slow, bureaucratic culture of GT. With tight functional silos and limited workspace, some of the staff even found themselves working in trailers in the parking lots. Furthermore, as the smallest division of GT, HVAC seldom got the attention that they needed from the top GT executives. One HVAC manager noted, "We were like the red-headed stepchild of GT."

Tracking the Progress

Our Organizational Culture Survey had been used by GT for four years before Tim Kuppler became GM of HVAC.[3] Given what he observed in the early days of his tenure as general manager, he believed that this approach could be helpful in diagnosing the division's problems and helpful in improving the business. The message from a survey of all the division's salaried employees in 2003 was clear. These survey results are presented in Figure 5.1. The results showed a weak sense of direction and a lot of uncertainty about the division's capabilities to make the changes required to become more competitive. They needed a sense of their future—and a plan for how they were going to get there.

Involvement Meetings

GT's approach for moving from diagnosis to action has important implications for every organization. They brought all salaried employees together for a day-long "involvement" meeting that

**Figure 5.1. 2003 Culture Survey Results:
HVAC North America**

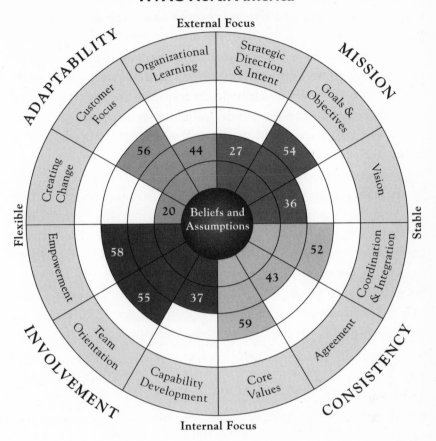

External Focus

Internal Focus

would serve as a platform for understanding the division's survey results and starting to plan the changes that would address their major problems.

From the beginning, there was pervasive skepticism. In the past, meetings of this type had led to few real changes. But Kuppler's enthusiasm for making HVAC North America a better place to work was infectious. Their first involvement meeting started with a review of HVAC history. After that, the leaders presented the culture model and the survey results. No one was surprised by the news that they had some work to do.

As a part of this meeting, the leadership team proposed a vision statement for the HVAC staff to consider. Small work groups then reacted to the proposed vision statement, offering suggestions on enhancing the customer relationship strategy and suggesting ways to address the issues raised by the survey. The process invited and rewarded everyone's participation in helping to determine the future strategic direction of the company. The ideas that came from these small-group discussions were presented to the entire group, with lots of suggestions for action steps and follow-up.

A few months later, a second involvement meeting was held to evaluate progress against the goals that they had set in the first meeting. Both management and employees were held responsible for formulating ideas and implementing change. As this cultural transformation started to gain momentum, attitudes started to shift throughout the organization. The involvement meetings became a twice-yearly event for employees, who started to look forward to these events as great opportunities to catch up with colleagues and contribute to shaping the future of the division.

Our Role at GT Automotive

We started doing consulting work at GT Automotive about four years before the work described in this chapter began. The Culture Survey was used extensively in the HVAC Division described in this chapter; it had more limited application in the other divisions of GT. We met with the executives and managers of GT to present results and facilitate the action planning process. By the time that the work described in this chapter began, GT was very familiar with our approach and managed this process very well themselves. In 2008, we completed an IMD teaching case on GT.

Source: Denison and Lief, 2009a and 2009b.

Business Teams

But involvement teams alone were not enough to drive the transformation. To sustain the momentum created by the involvement
meetings, the next step was to capture that energy and direct
it at a set of core business issues. To do this, they created a
set of business teams focused on the specific changes required
to enhance the customer experience at HVAC. Five business
teams were created, ranging from five to twenty individuals,
and every salaried employee was involved in the work of at
least one of those teams. They thought through the choices
for the best structure, composition, goals, responsibilities, and
metrics of each of the new business teams. Leadership selection and operating procedures were left to the discretion of
each team. The only requirements for each team were that they
should: (1) meet regularly, to encourage communication and
engagement; (2) participate in a charity function annually; (3)
update their objectives on a quarterly basis; (4) report progress
at monthly business meetings; and (5) maintain a site on the
company intranet. To keep each other informed, the business
teams were invited to present their best practices and current
challenges at monthly all-team meetings.

These business teams overlapped quite a bit with the existing
organizational structure. But their purpose was not just to have
every department form a business team; rather, it was to create
a new way of working, in keeping with the overall purpose of
"enhancing the customer experience at HVAC." One important
feature of this approach was that the business teams were *not*
simply the leadership teams of the departments or units. Instead,
the members of the business team were usually one or two levels
down in the organization from the leaders of the department
in which the business team was being formed. This "action
team" approach is usually very effective, because it creates a
team of knowledgeable and experienced individuals with a strong
stake in leading the organization into the future, rather than an

intact leadership team that may be tempted to get distracted by defending the decisions of the past.

After a year of this process, the leadership team and the staff were actually a little surprised by their progress. Their 2004 survey results, presented in Figure 5.2, showed substantial improvements in every category. HVAC beat their profit plan by 20 percent in 2004, and quality and safety performance also improved. The efforts of Kuppler and his team drew the notice of TI corporate executives. They had created a cultural transformation of their own and had led a significant turnaround in the business. HVAC was no longer the "red-headed stepchild" of TI.

Figure 5.2. 2004 Culture Survey Results: HVAC North America

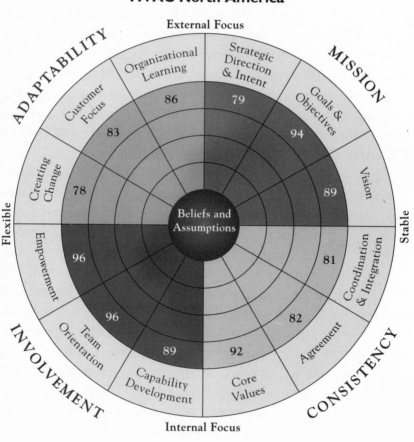

Be Careful What You Wish For

As a result of these successes, Kuppler was asked by TI to take on global responsibility as vice president and general manager for the HVAC Division. Although he was convinced that he needed to implement a change agenda in his new position, he wondered if he should take the same approach in this new context. Corporate culture would clearly be an issue, but this time national culture would be too. In his new global role, he would have to deal with the complexity of HVAC's operations in eleven countries around the world. The workforce was scattered over a wide geographic area, and the influence of diverging national cultures on the corporate culture would make the job much more difficult.

His initial idea was to extend the successful change process that they had used in North America but to continuously modify it based on the lessons they learned in each country. Europe was clearly the top priority. HVAC had manufacturing operations in Spain, Italy, and the Czech Republic, with commercial operations headquartered in Heidelberg, Germany. There were big cultural differences among these locations. Would the same approach that brought an enhanced work environment and impressive financial performance in the United States also prevail in this diverse set of European settings?

Kuppler sensed that the strength of the European organization was in its disciplined approach, respect for authority, and dedication to following through on tasks. However, he also found that employees seemed very skeptical of new initiatives and, therefore, less willing to candidly share their feelings and ideas. This group needed convincing that real change would come, no matter what they did or how much they talked. But this time the job was also more complex because of the five operating languages that were used in the European facilities. He had his work cut out for him, but he had the strong support of the global HVAC leadership team he had created with representatives from around the division. Table 5.1 presents a summary of the similarities and differences between the United States and Europe.

Table 5.1. North America/Europe Culture Change Comparison: GT Automotive HVAC

	Strengths	Issues	Culture Change Key Elements	Culture Change Marketing and Initial Implementation
North America	• Quick to accept the need for change • Team spirit builds quickly and leads to increased discipline and commitment • Open to sharing ideas and criticism	• Strong desire for team coordination and motivation • Critical and sarcastic • Initial lack of discipline and organization; poor follow-through on commitments • Quick to turn negative with lack of communication • Easily bored with plans and details	• Implementation of team structures • Alignment of vision, strategy, objectives, metrics, and rewards • Denison survey and formal corrective actions • Involvement meetings and business stream meetings • Implementation of extensive capability development processes • Regular communication and team activities	• Emphasize key facts to make the case for change • Management implements small changes based on employee feedback to build momentum • Extensive team activities to build team spirit • More extensive team reviews and support, with emphasis on team commitments • Very regular recognition activities of all sizes to maintain interest and support • Use of humor and stories to combat sarcasm and maintain interest

Europe			
• Disciplined and organized • High respect for order and authority • Excellent follow-through on commitments	• Skeptical • Tentative to share ideas with senior managers • Team spirit builds when commitments are met • Change accepted only with clear explanation, planning, and initial follow-through • More significant accomplishments required to motivate	• Same	• Thoroughly justify the case for change and the processes for driving change • Emphasize more substantial management commitments and timing to gain respect when met • Team activities start slowly and grow over time • Management involvement to encourage sharing of ideas • Emphasize major recognition activities with more detail about plans, commitments, and accomplishments

Figure 5.3. 2004 Culture Survey Results: HVAC Europe

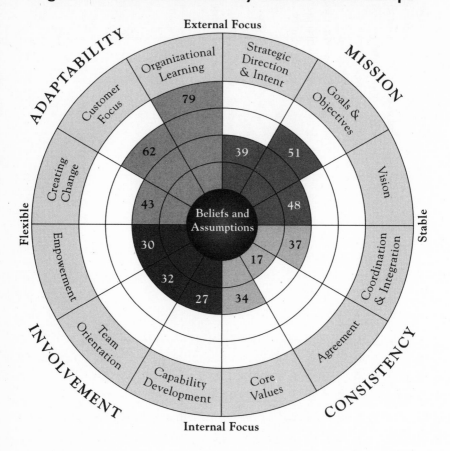

The survey results for Europe in 2004, presented in Figure 5.3, were actually more challenging than the initial survey results in North America in 2003. Consistency, which was not so much of a problem for North America, turned out to be the weakest trait for Europe, reflecting that there was little agreement among the different locations about what was needed to create one global HVAC business. The survey results were available in June 2004 and the first involvement meetings were scheduled for that same month. Once again, the agenda for the meeting included the presentation of the group's results and votes on establishing priorities for action plans. A vision and strategy for the European unit was discussed and clarified. The next meeting was scheduled for November 2004.

The reaction to these results varied quite a bit by location. In the commercial center in Heidelberg, home to the sales teams and the design groups, there was a lot of skepticism about the results and their implications for change. In their first involvement meeting, it took a long time to gain a consensus to move forward. But once they had reached an agreement, the Germans tended to move forward with discipline and structure. The manufacturing locations in Italy, Spain, and the Czech Republic, in contrast, had initial discussions that were more receptive to the results and the need to take action. Their consensus came more quickly, but their follow-through was less structured.

The low scores on agreement that appeared in their results pointed to a set of issues that could not be resolved using a location-by-location approach. This led to a series of discussions among managers from the four locations about coordination and agreement between the customer, the sales process, the design team, and the manufacturing sites. This kind of discussion had never happened before. It forced them to sort out issues that had several layers of culture. With the Germans, the Italians, the Spaniards, and the Czechs all in the room, there were several layers of culture to consider: the center versus the locations, sales versus manufacturing, design versus production, Northern versus Southern Europe, and Germany versus the rest. All of these factors had an important influence on the values of the team members and their ability to work together. Nonetheless, these discussions led to a set of cross-functional metrics—such as launch quality, sales, and margins—that forced a new level of collaboration in the European organization.

As in North America, Kuppler worked quickly with his leadership team to create business teams throughout Europe to follow up on the momentum created by the involvement meetings. In all, thirty business teams were established across the global business unit by the time he was finished. A summary

Table 5.2. HVAC Global Business Teams

Global	North America
Core Engineering	GM
Technology	DCx
Commercial	Delphi
Business Systems	Air International
Purchasing	Ford
Estimating	Prototype
Europe	Employee Involvement
GM / Fiat / Suzuki	Design
Strategic Customers	Tool Group
Tier 1 + Truck	Plants: 1, 2, 3, 4, 7, Service
Customers	Sanford Plant
Jablonec Plant	*Asia*
Tauste Plant	Asia Commercial
Cisliano Plant	Anting, China Plant

of the global business teams that were created is presented in Table 5.2. Each of the teams was required to develop a standard set of metrics that they would use to report their progress on a regular basis. Each team was also required to update everyone through their team webpage on the company intranet. Although this process had many similarities with the process used in the United States, it was also very flexible. Kuppler noted,

> This was not a tightly planned effort from the start. It was more watching how things evolved over time and continuously obtaining employee feedback for improvement as we defined and updated our priorities. We learned what to emphasize as we went along. And we got a better appreciation for how culture touches everything.

The changes from 2004 to 2005 were dramatic. Much improvement was noted, with better results in every category.

There was still much to be done, particularly in the area of Consistency—Core Values, Agreement, and Coordination and Integration—but overall the leadership team had much to feel good about. As reflected in Figure 5.4, HVAC operations in Europe moved forward in a variety of ways. There were signs of progress in everything from financial performance to new business wins to safety, quality, and strategy implementation.

Kuppler came to believe that the only way to survive as a firm in the auto industry was to strengthen the team, building individual leadership capabilities through regular feedback for senior managers, routine developmental reviews for all managers, exchange programs between locations, and a significant expansion of the opportunities for training and development. But it was also important to line up behind one comprehensive, well-understood vision. Regular follow-up and communication with respect to progress toward that vision was also important in order to sustain the effort. These changes led to considerable improvement in the performance of the business and made TI a healthier, more enjoyable place to work. Table 5.3 gives an overview of the changes in performance that occurred between 2002 and 2006.

After successfully leading the HVAC business transformation in North America and Europe, Kuppler went on to head TI's entire operation in North America, with responsibility for the brake and fuel business as well as the HVAC Division. He introduced his leadership and teamwork ideas to this work unit as well. In mid-2008, following the appointment of a new corporate CEO and the implementation of a new global organizational structure, Kuppler left TI. But looking back on his efforts, he reflected,

> The most important factor in our success was the freedom given to me and our leadership team by my boss, Rich Kolpasky. He had confidence in me and my ideas. He trusted me to run the businesses the way I thought best. After reading literally hundreds of leadership and management books, I had ideas

Figure 5.4. Comparing 2004 to 2005 Culture Survey Results: HVAC Europe

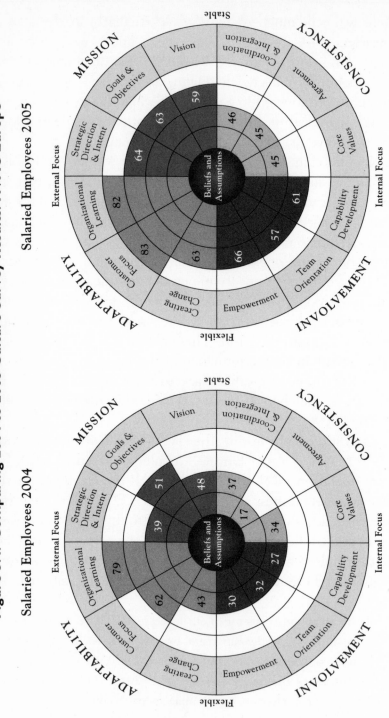

Salaried Employees 2005

Salaried Employees 2004

Table 5.3. Improved HVAC Culture = Improved Results

	2002	*2003–2006*
Profit	On plan	2003–2005: 10 percent better than plan 2006: NA restructuring
Quality	Thirty-seven parts per million (PPM)	Single-digit PPM
New Business Wins	Two non-GM wins in prior five years	Over 20 non-GM wins
Globalization	No Asia presence	Four programs won in Asia New plant established in China
Global Leadership	Eight leaders in five years	One leader
Global Coordination	None	Leading TI business Global strategies Global teams Global intranet Global business processes Global product designs Global manufacturing processes

I wanted to try out. He gave me the opportunity to follow my instincts and knowledge. And the results were satisfying—a more involved workforce and substantially improved performance when we initially managed the culture change.

Lessons for Leaders

GT Automotive's success, using a change process that was first developed in the United States and then applied in Europe, came as quite a surprise to the organization and to industry observers. Isn't national culture supposed to be a nearly insurmountable barrier to creating a truly "organizational culture"? Doesn't each national culture require its own independent approach to creating the buy-in required for successful organizational change? Let's consider some of these questions as we look at lessons that we can take away from this example.

Do What You Know Best

Although it is clearly true that different national contexts may require very different approaches to organizational change, this case is a good reminder of the fact that doing what you know how to do with honesty, openness, and integrity can go a long way. Leading with curiosity, respect, and a clear set of principles that you are trying to apply in the new context can be quite successful.

When we use an approach that is familiar to us, we are able to more quickly create a structure that will apply some core principles to have a large-scale impact. In the United States, Kuppler created a structure of weekly business team meetings, monthly business meetings, quarterly objective updates, quarterly global strategy meetings, and twice a year an involvement meeting with a social event in the evening. This set of activities reinforced the change process and created a new level of teamwork. This architecture allowed the organizations in both locations to manage the transition from the insights and dialogue of the involvement meetings to the action orientation of the business teams.

The logic of this approach and the credibility that it had based on the success in North America provided an irresistible advantage to the change process. It didn't take a lot of time to gear up, and Kuppler and his colleagues were very familiar with the key leverage points in the process as it unfolded. The integrity of this structured approach seemed to outweigh the needs for a more unique approach to each country and location.

But Adapt as You Go

On the other hand, it is very important to understand that the lessons about "doing what you know best" were about expressing the same set of principles in the new European context, and not about enforcing adherence to TI's practices on the ground. There is a big difference between consistency and compliance. One interesting example of this was the reaction to the "service learning" component of the change process in the United States and Europe. In the United States, spending a day together as a team working on a charity was a big part of the process. It built a commitment among the team members that they were a force for good and that they were working together for a purpose that went beyond their quarterly business targets. But in Europe, for a number of reasons, this component of the process was not as well received. So they changed this part of the process and concentrated their efforts on other ways to build teamwork and commitment.

It is also critically important to remember that expecting to find a uniform approach to the change process is mostly wishful thinking. Change almost always happens at different rates in different places. As seductive as it may seem to roll out a global change process with the expectation of a unified approach, it almost never happens. Consistency in the change process is often worth striving for, but it seldom happens. Change strategies designed to create momentum will beat change strategies designed to create uniformity every time.

Exporting Culture Change: Beyond GT Automotive

GT provides us with lots of good examples of the challenges of exporting change across national boundaries. It is hard work, but as this case shows, it is definitely possible. So despite the hard work associated with leading global culture change, organizations keep trying to overcome the realities of fragmented, disconnected "global" organizations to try to create better integration. Let's consider some other authors' perspectives on this issue.

Which Is Stronger: National Culture or Organizational Culture?

As many authors have noted, national cultures have a depth that organizational cultures can never achieve.[4] It takes hundreds or even thousands of years to develop a national culture, and that process creates roots that go far deeper than any that could ever be created by an organization.[5] However, Freud reminds us that "love and work are the cornerstones of humanity." He didn't mention anything about which passport we carry!

There is no question that nationality has an influence on those all-important work habits that are so central to our identities. But our habits are also shaped by many other aspects of the context that we work in: the organization we join, the industry we work in, the profession we have chosen, and the work group we are a part of. All of these factors have a strong influence on our identities—as the following situation illustrates.

Two poets walk into a bar, followed by two engineers. One of the poets is French and the other is English. Same with the engineers. The four of them start talking. What do you think will have the biggest influence on the approach that they take to the issues they discuss: their nationality or their profession? What if they are talking about building a bridge? Or writing a song? How about EU fiscal policy?

The answer, of course, is that this depends on *the issues they are discussing*. But when it comes to organizational culture, many of the values, beliefs, and work practices that we develop are quite specific to the organizational context that we work in.[6] Occupational culture, for example, is also a strong influence. It is always fascinating to see the reaction of a roomful of executives from all over the world when they are grouped by function. There is almost a sigh of relief that now auditors can talk to auditors, pilots can talk to pilots, engineers can talk to engineers, and sales guys can talk to sales guys. The influence of nationality on work habits fades away fast.[7]

These connections of common organizational experience provide a basis for creating a change process that spans national boundaries. Lessons learned in one country can sometimes be transferred across boundaries to build momentum for change.[8] National culture has a strong influence on the way that we organize and the way that we lead. But it is certainly not the only influence.

Clear Direction Makes All the Difference

The lessons from this chapter are also a good reminder that setting a clear direction has a strong influence. A long debate over the right or the wrong way to proceed is seldom a motivator. Interestingly enough, setting a clear direction is so important to a team, a group, or an organization that the energy and focus can sometimes transcend the importance of the actual direction itself. Scholar Karl Weick tells this story:

> The young lieutenant of a small Hungarian detachment in the Alps sent a reconnaissance unit into the icy wilderness. It began to snow immediately, snowed for two days and the unit did not return. The lieutenant suffered, fearing that he had dispatched his own people to their death. The third day the unit came back. Where had they been? How had they made their way?
>
> Yes, they said, we considered ourselves lost and waited for the end. And then one of us found a map in his pocket. That calmed us down. We pitched camp, lasted out the snowstorm, and then with the map, we discovered our bearings. And here we are.
>
> The lieutenant borrowed this remarkable map and had a good look at it. He discovered to his astonishment that it was not a map of the Alps, but a map of the Pyrenees.[9]

Setting direction and building momentum are essential to any change process. Momentum can build across national boundaries if we follow those elements of the culture that we share in common—and respect those elements of the culture that we do not.

6

BUILDING A GLOBAL BUSINESS *IN* AN EMERGING MARKET

Established corporations typically enter emerging markets for three main reasons: First, they want to sell their products to a large and growing population that has an increasing need for their products and an increasing ability to pay for them. So, when Siemens of Germany entered the Chinese market for high-speed trains, they were lured by the Chinese plans to create the most advanced railway infrastructure in the world. It worked! China now has the largest network of high-speed trains in the world, and has an aggressive plan expanding their rail infrastructure like no other country in the world.[1] Germany's Siemens, along with Japan's Kawasaki, France's Alstom, and Canada's Bombardier, are the major suppliers to the Chinese market.

The second major reason that mature market corporations enter emerging markets is to reduce the costs of labor and other factors of production. So when a European IT company moves its software development to India, or when an American textile company closes an old mill in Puerto Rico and opens a new one in Vietnam, they do so to reduce labor costs, even through their primary markets may remain in Europe or the States. This often leads them to the third major reason that corporations enter emerging markets: so they can use their operations in that market as an export platform to serve other countries as well.

But when corporations begin to *combine* these approaches, the process of entering an emerging market becomes far more complex. Producing products for local consumption requires an increased investment in marketing, sales, and distribution. It may also become more difficult to protect their technology on the ground. New products have to be developed to meet the demands of local consumers. Choices about ownership, control, and legal structure lead to joint ventures, alliances, partnerships, and acquisitions. These decisions also move things along to the point where the local, emerging market operations have an integrated role in a global corporate strategy.

Inevitably, the last pieces of the puzzle to be integrated into the local environment in an emerging market are the capabilities of research, development, and design. Taking this step requires a level of integration that is difficult to achieve and doesn't come without years of hard work to develop the mindset, capabilities, and methods for global collaboration.

Although it is tempting to assume that a globalization strategy can be pursued by focusing primarily on things such as foreign direct investment, legal structures, ownership interests, IP protection strategies, and supply-chain management, in reality the globalization journey is perhaps the biggest cultural adventure of all. And the stakes are very high. Just consider one fact: When General Motors declared bankruptcy in June 2009, their one-billion-plus shares of stock were worth less than a dollar a share. But that year they sold nearly two million cars in China.[2] Do the math. Even a year or two later, when their stock had rebounded into the thirties, the value of the total corporation was not much more than the value of the business that they had created in China over the preceding ten to fifteen years.

Building a Business in an Emerging Market

The choice to build a business in an emerging market is one of the most important decisions that a corporation can make. The cycle starts with developing sales and marketing capabilities and production operations. Managing the added sales or reduced costs from entering an emerging market doesn't pose much of a challenge to the global strategy of most firms. But the path from this point to the point when the local operation plays a key role in implementing an integrated global strategy is a demanding one. Let's consider the case of GE Heathcare's efforts to build their Chinese business from a base near Shanghai.[3]

Leading with a Vision

GE Healthcare first entered the Chinese market in 1991. The story that we tell in this chapter focuses on their efforts to build their anesthesia business. Globally, GE's serious efforts in the anesthesia business began with their 2002 acquisition of Finland's Datex-Ohmeda (D-O), the leading global brand in anesthesia equipment. D-O had sold a limited number of their high-end machines in China prior to the acquisition, but after the acquisition they started production of D-O equipment in Wuxi at the GE Healthcare site.

Anesthesia machines are essential in the operating room: They provide both anesthesia and oxygen to patients during surgery. GE estimated that this market would grow by 8 to 10 percent per year, in part because China's rural health reform was about to bring 80 percent of the rural population—nearly seven hundred million people—into the national health insurance system.

GE's efforts in the Chinese market accelerated with their 2006 acquisition of Zymed, a family-run company also based in Wuxi. Zymed, which GE renamed Clinical Systems Wuxi (CSW) after the acquisition, manufactured and sold anesthesia machines and respirators with technology that had been "adapted" from D-O's technologies. Zymed was the market leader in the Chinese low-end domestic anesthesia machine market, with an estimated market share of 20 to 25 percent. GE later folded D-O into CSW to create the performance segment of their anesthesia business.

Zymed was founded in 1988 by the head of the Chong family. Ten years later, his four grandchildren took over the business and developed it into the market leader. Each of the grandchildren was an excellent salesperson. They divided the China market into four regions, and each took responsibility for one region. In 2004 and 2005, they sold around 900 machines each year; the number reached 1,200 units in 2006, the year Zymed was acquired by GE Healthcare. Guo Song, operations manager of CSW, commented: "The organization structure of Zymed was simple. It had dreams, but no long-term strategy. It had a culture of thrift. It also had good execution, which was based on a transparent rewards system. In its ten-year history, employees benefited a lot financially."

But like many Chinese family-run companies, Zymed did not pay much attention to internal controls. There was little vision and few control systems. The incumbent general manager had devoted most of his time to sales and marketing, but hadn't created a strategic plan for building the global value-segment anesthesia business. This might not have mattered so much in a fast-growing market in which demand always exceeded supply. But when GE Healthcare decided to buy Zymed, quality quickly became an issue. At one point, they had to stop shipping machines because of customer complaints and quality problems. In addition, their market share was also shrinking because they had downsized their distribution channels to ensure compliance with GE's internal quality guidelines.

So in the second half of 2007, GE appointed Matti Lehtonen as the new general manager of the business. In many ways, from a cultural standpoint Lehtonen was a perfect choice for the GM job. He had grown up in Finland, was trained as an engineer, and had worked with D-O in the past. But he had spent the last twenty-five years in China working in electronics manufacturing and was fluent in Mandarin, Portuguese, and German as well as Finnish and English.

Building the Management Team

Lehtonen soon rebuilt the management team and included a full complement of GE veterans. For example, Maggie Zhang, operations director, had been with GE Healthcare for over ten years, and Zhang Yukun, global sourcing manager, had seven years of GE experience under his belt. Lehtonen also recruited a new finance manager from GE Healthcare China and an HR manager with long GE experience. These team members had a strong identification with GE values, which was essential to the next stage of integration: injecting a strong sense of vision, mission, and strategy into the organization and reshaping the mindset of all employees. These managers also had experience in managing the requirements that came from GE headquarters. Their global sourcing manager noted: "A lot of requirements come from EHS [environment, health, and safety], HR, finance, and other functions. GE culture is very aggressive. You must close lots of things within a very short period of time."

A Vision-Led Strategy

Lehtonen and his team formulated a vision for CSW and worked out a strategy map, linking the long-term goals of CSW with its operational activities and short-term imperatives. He then worked with the management to create maps for key functions, such as sales and marketing, operations, and engineering. Then they created action plans for the implementation of the strategy maps. The next step was to promote these ideas throughout the company. They convened monthly town hall meetings that involved all employees. At every monthly and quarterly staff meeting and other management events, Lehtonen and his management team reiterated the vision, the mission, and the GE values and continued to refine their strategy maps.

Matti also used some "special tools." On both sides of his office door, he put up Chinese poetic couplets, which translated as "Pressure Is Motivation," "Hard Work Is Happiness," and "Serve the Patient." The couplets caught everyone's attention, and for Chinese employees, it was interesting and unique to see the traditional couplets outside the office door of a foreign general manager. His office was located near the entry of the office area, so every employee passed by his office each day as they arrived and left.

To demonstrate the kinds of behaviors that were desired and promoted, the management team presented many awards to their people at all kinds of occasions. For example, they gave an award to a cross-functional team, which included people from sourcing, engineering, and operations, when they solved a quality problem in record time, ensuring on-time delivery to their customer. The leaders sent a clear signal that the award was intended to promote: (1) customer and quality priority, (2) cross-functional cooperation, (3) willingness to work hard, and (4) the attitude of making impossible things possible. These priorities also fit well with GE's five growth traits (external focus, clear thinker, inclusiveness, expertise, and imagination). The top priority was external focus, which meant customer and quality were on the top of the list. This focus on quality was a big change from the old sales-oriented Zymed culture.

Tracking the Progress

GE Healthcare used our Organizational Culture Survey in late 2007 and early 2009 to track their progress. The results from late 2007, a few months after Lehtonen came on board, are presented in Figure 6.1 for three groups at CSW: Operations, Managerial and Supervisory, and R&D.

These results present some interesting contrasts. The management scores are the lowest across the board, which appears to reflect the management team's impatience with the status quo and their perception that they had a *long* way to go on customer focus. Vision and learning were their highest scores, reflecting some of the priorities they had pursued in the first few months. Like many Chinese companies, they also saw capability development as one of the areas most in need of improvement.

The profiles for R&D and Operations are somewhat better, but many of the same priorities for improvement appear. After

Figure 6.1. 2007 Culture Survey Results: GE Healthcare, Clinical Systems Wuxi (CSW)

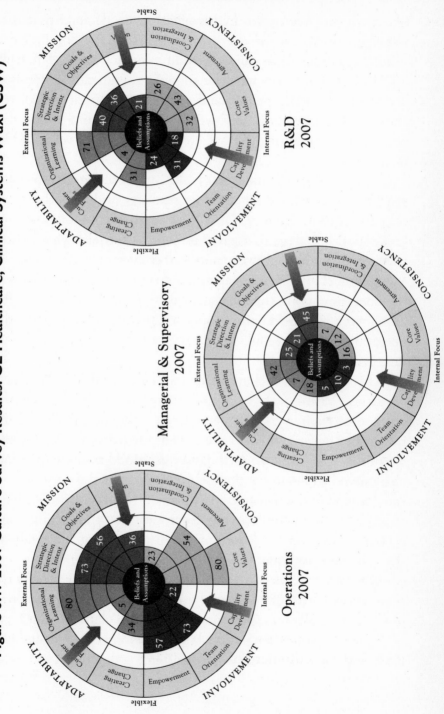

extensive discussion, the management team decided that they wanted to focus on three major priorities for the coming year: vision, customer focus, and capability development. When we asked Matti Lehtonen what he thought this meant in terms of action priorities, he paused and said, "I think that one of the things that it means is that we should devote more time and resources to something that we are already doing." What did he mean by that?

To reshape the mindset of all employees, and especially the engineers who designed the products and had the main responsibility for quality, CSW had been sending engineers in groups to hospital operating rooms to see with their own eyes how their products helped doctors save the lives of patients. Kevin Meng, a mechanical engineer, said with emotion, "When I was in the operating room, the idea occurred to me that if the machine didn't work, we could harm people. On the other hand, when the operations are successful, I feel proud of my job because I help save people's lives."

This one intervention touched all three of the CSW action priorities. Visiting an operating room not only clarified the purpose of their work but also clarified the complexity of the network of customers that they served: the patients, the doctors, the nurses, the hospital, and the insurers. In addition, this program also proved to be an invaluable investment in the capability of their engineers and became a key part of their recruiting strategy to attract new engineers to the organization. Other action plans and priorities also came out of their discussions of the results in the management team, the staff, and the town hall meetings.

Over the following year, CSW changed dramatically. As the results from early 2009 in Figure 6.2 show, they made great progress in almost all areas. But notably, they also clarified their focus on their biggest challenge, capability development. Especially in R&D and engineering, CSW was in a fierce competition for talent.

> ## Our Role at GE Healthcare China
>
> Our work with GE Healthcare China began in 2007, when newly appointed Managing Director Matti Lehtonen attended a conference that we organized in Shanghai. From there, we worked with him to organize a process that would help with the transformation he had planned. We met with the leadership team to debrief the results and helped facilitate their planning meeting. We also did an extensive set of interviews in the organization, in English and Chinese, to understand the organization and the transformation they were trying to achieve. We wrote an IMD teaching case on GE Healthcare China that was published in 2009.

One Culture? Or Three?

The discussion of the survey results once again focused the company's attention on the four different groups of people who made up the organization: the old D-O culture, the old Zymed culture, the GE culture, and those newly hired from the outside. For those from the D-O culture, joining CSW seemed like a step down—the CSW product line was focused on the value-segment and the machines were not nearly as sophisticated, or as expensive, as the former D-O line. Those from Zymed were not accustomed to processes and systems and felt like these demands slowed them down at every turn. They were more sales-oriented, resourceful, and entrepreneurial—and also more accustomed to waiting for instructions from their bosses. The GE veterans among them struggled to think through how to keep the business running while bringing it into compliance with GE's global guidelines for process discipline and quality. The newcomers? They were often disoriented and a bit confused with the complexity of the situation.

Figure 6.2. Comparing 2007 to 2009 Culture Survey Results: GE Healthcare, Clinical Systems Wuxi (CSW)

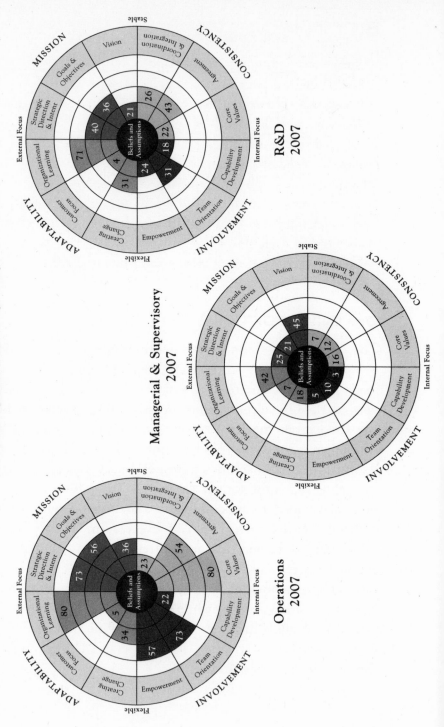

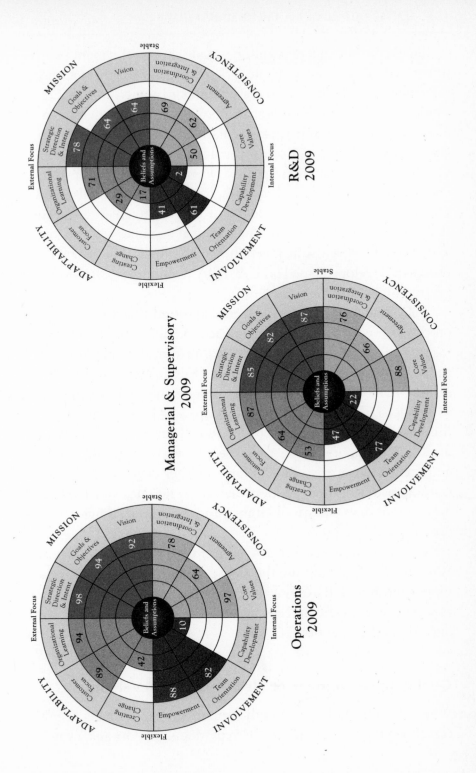

R&D
2009

Managerial & Supervisory
2009

Operations
2009

Juggling three different cultures made the development of an integrated process very difficult. There were at least three strong influences on any attempt to create a standard unified process. GE, a process leader, had strong global efforts under way to create common processes among all of its subsidiaries. D-O, a leading brand in the anesthesia business, had its own advanced process discipline, which was quite different from the new unified GE process. Zymed had few clearly articulated processes, but it had a well-established way of doing things. This made it very difficult to create a "clean slate" advantage. Kevin Wu, a mechanical engineer who worked with Zymed before the acquisition, commented, "The new [GE] process is developed based on U.S. FDA requirements. Its level is just too high for our low baseline."

Lucy Jing, engineering manager, admitted that the new GE process slowed down the working pace of engineers, though she insisted the process would be an advantage in the long run. But the new process did frustrate engineers. Kevin Wu said, "It seems no one realizes how much a good process means to engineers. My understanding is that a good process is like a signpost on the highway. With a good process, you'll know clearly how to do things...Engineers are those people who like to ask 'why?' and find the answer...But we have neither clear signposts nor people answering the question here...sometimes you have to spend more than a day to do something that can be done in one hour without the process."

Kevin Meng, a mechanical engineer from D-O, echoed Kevin Wu's words: "We can't use the D-O process, as it doesn't have a supporting system here. But the new process is not clear. When you get lost with the process and ask someone else, it seems no one knows the direction."

Quality Improvement or New Product Development?

With a large installed base of the former Zymed products, CSW continued to sell and service these products. The former Zymed engineers had initially imitated the design of the D-O products without understanding all of the underlying design principles. So it was difficult, if not impossible, to trace the problems back to the original blueprints. Thus, whenever they received a customer complaint, it went to the engineering department. The engineers had to figure out what the problem was and develop a solution.

For GE Healthcare and CSW, every customer complaint was a serious issue. This meant that quality issues consumed most of the engineering resources and compromised the engineers' product development efforts. Engineering Manager Lucy Jing said, "We have to put about 90 percent of our engineering resources on maintenance. If I could start from scratch and put the 90 percent of the engineering resources on new product development, we could reduce quality issues by 80 percent."

But CSW just could not just put aside customer orders and customer complaints. Nor could they simply allocate more engineering resources to new product development. Although GE was supportive of the business, actually getting approval for a new head count was difficult. Even when they did, it was difficult to attract talented, experienced engineers to Wuxi—a second-tier city of only five million people, two hours' drive from Shanghai. CSW had started to develop new products, but the pace was slow due to the lack of engineering resources. Project Leader Google Wu summarized their progress: "We have milestones for new product design, from M0 to M5. Now our new product is at M0, the stage for collecting information, defining products to meet market needs."

Toward a Global Strategy

Despite all of the struggles, in 2008 CSW managed to double their sales volume in terms of units installed in hospitals over their 2007 sales volume. Exports to India and increasingly to China and Russia had grown to 40 percent of their total volume. Progress on a new anesthesia machine that would create the foundation for a global, value-segment equipment business was slow, but by 2010 CSW had introduced their new "9100c" model and was shipping this to emerging markets all over the world. Although this machine still did not meet the FDA requirements necessary for the U.S. or Western European markets, it was a massive step forward and laid the foundation for resolving the quality and process problems that CSW needed to address to build a global business from a base in Wuxi.

Lessons for Leaders

Within five to six years, GE Healthcare made dramatic progress in China. They established a strong position in the local market and then started an export business, focusing first on India and Brazil and then on Russia. Building from these accomplishments, they played an increasingly important role in the global anesthesia business by establishing Wuxi as the center of the value segment in the anesthesia business and developing new products to serve the global value segment from that base. The leader of this business, Matti Lehtonen, was then promoted to lead GE's global anesthesia business. Let's look at some of the lessons that we can learn from their progress.

Vision Wins Again

As with several of the other stories, this case is a strong testament to the power of a compelling vision. At the beginning, Lehtonen's choice to lead with vision—rather than strategy, process, quality, or sales—was not necessarily a popular or a well-understood decision. Many of the staff in Wuxi, as well as executives in other parts of GE, questioned the wisdom of this approach and were often impatient with the time spent talking about the vision in their town hall meetings.

But the time spent on the vision actually proved to be essential to the transformation. The common purpose that they articulated in their town hall meetings gave a *reason* for the future strategy of the business. It gave a reason for integrating the production processes for D-O and Zymed. It gave a reason for the urgency of resolving their quality problems as quickly as possible, at the same time that they were striving to accomplish product upgrades and a complete product redesign. The vision helped them make sense of the intense mix of short-term and long-term priorities that they faced. Longer term, this focus on the vision also created the foundation for Wuxi to lead the value segment of the global anesthesia business.

At the beginning it was very difficult to devote the time to a long-term vision. It was even harder to devote the time to the town hall meetings when the urgent quality problems of the day were still unresolved. But in the end this strategic choice paid off handsomely. A little vision often goes a long, long way.

Organizational Subcultures Are Everywhere

In many ways, the biggest cultural hurdle to overcome was not the global challenge of an American multinational building a business in China. Rather, it was the challenge of bridging the gap between the organizational cultures of Datex-Ohmeda and Zymed. Both of these organizations were Chinese, but they were as different as a Silicon Valley start-up and a Rust Belt manufacturer, and they had a history of being competitors. Keeping both operations running while integrating them into one was the fundamental challenge. Without succeeding at this first step, none of the rest would have been possible.

The "American" part of this cultural mix is also very interesting. At the beginning of this story, the GE global standards seemed highly ambitious, if not totally unattainable. Managing the relationship with corporate headquarters mostly meant a lot of administrative work to comply with the corporate standard. But GE's FDA-driven standard was, in the end, critically important to bringing D-O and Zymed together. Without the GE standard, there would have been no common point on the horizon toward which both D-O and Zymed could evolve. There are many aspects to the American culture besides GE's process discipline, but that was certainly the aspect of "American" business culture that had the biggest impact in Wuxi.

It's extremely important to understand national differences in work habits and organizational cultures. But if there is one strong argument against the dominant force of national culture in determining workplace relations, it is the huge variety of organizations, each with *their* own unique culture, that exists in every country in the world. Individual organizations have unique histories and contexts, and they grow in unique ways. And within each of those unique organizations there is a unique mix of subcultures within cultures that are a key part of the logic by which the parts fit together. This all adds to the complexity. All Chinese organizations are no more alike than all American organizations or all Swiss organizations. So it is essential to focus on the unique aspects of each individual firm as we move around the world and to pay attention to the individual subcultures within them.

Acquiring a "Competitor"

One of the most interesting parts of this case is the fact that when GE acquired Zymed to expand into the Chinese market, they were actually purchasing a company that had originally "adapted" its technology from D-O.[4] Zymed then further developed this technology to fit the Chinese market. This was an unusual acquisition strategy, although not without precedent. The upside of this strategy is clear: It was attractive to eliminate an imitator and a competitor in the local market, and it was also attractive to quickly gain the market presence and distribution network that Zymed had established. An organic growth strategy would have taken much longer.

And in the end, surprisingly few of the integration challenges stemmed from Zymed's "adapting" of the D-O technology. By the time Zymed was acquired by GE, there were enough differences in the technology that the situation still required the definition of a new set of GE-based design and production principles. This suggests that, beyond the usual challenges of merging two organizations that had been competitors in the past, GE paid no real penalty—nor gained much real benefit based on the prior connection between Zymed and D-O technologies.

Building a Global Business in an Emerging Market: Beyond GE Healthcare

The study of how multinational firms expand in emerging markets has a long history. But within the past decade, this expansion process has accelerated dramatically. This increase in speed and complexity has put a premium on a company's ability to manage cultural change and integration. The clash of core beliefs and values and daily work practices has become a part of the daily routine.

The capability to manage cultural complexity is a powerful force. When harnessed, it can be the crucial element in creating a global corporate culture. When ignored, cultural fragmentation can become a major barrier to both strategic and operational integration.

The Theory of Globalization: From the Past to the Future

Past approaches to globalization have pointed to three distinct stages of entering a new market—ownership, location, and internalization.[5] These stages are often used to describe the evolution of a firm's globalization strategy and their specific approach to entering an individual market. Firms often start to enter an emerging market by exporting from their base in a mature market. Their next step is to move to ownership—they acquire a firm in that market or create a firm to represent their business there. The next stage after ownership is localization, as the firm gradually moves production and later engineering and local design functions to an emerging market, to either serve that market or serve as a base to export from that market. During the final stage, internalization, the firm moves toward creating an integrated operation in the emerging market.

But today, these basic economic decisions tell us very little about a firm's chances for success in an emerging market. Ownership is important in an emerging market to establish the firm's presence and commitment and to gain access to local resources. Location is important too. A firm doesn't need to own everything or to be on every street corner in every emerging market, but firms can no longer achieve a visible presence without creating strong local organizations.

The third stage, internalization, has become much more important to global expansion than it has been in the past. The quality of internalization has become the critical frontier of globalization. Global corporations must demonstrate the superiority of their approach to building a local organization. The quality of that organization is what will determine the success of the firm.

Consider the experience of Pfizer in China and their joint venture with Shanghai Pharmaceutical. This past decade, Pfizer took the lead among pharmaceutical companies to establish an R&D base in Shanghai. Many companies have tried to avoid revealing their critical research capabilities in China in order to protect their intellectual property. But more recently, Pfizer has moved all of their antibacterial research to this location. Why do they continue to invest in this way? There are many attractions, but perhaps the most compelling factor is the incredible stream of life science graduates that China will produce this coming decade. Other pharmaceutical companies—such as GSK, Novo Nordisk, and Sanofi-Aventis—have also followed this path. This trend points to the importance to Western firms of insourcing world-class knowledge workers, not just outsourcing low-wage manufacturing jobs.

Or consider GE's John F. Welch Technology Centre in Bangalore, founded in 2000. GE saw the limits of outsourcing and started to build their own technology centers that could provide them with all of the advantages of India's market for knowledge workers. Ultimately, the success of these strategies depends on the ability of multinational firms to become global "magnets" for top talent. As they develop the capability to compete for top talent and use that talent to build key components of their global organizations in emerging markets, they will establish themselves as global leaders.

Culture as a Competitive Advantage

In the early days of the culture movement, researchers pointed out that the unique culture of a firm was one of its most important resources.[6] It takes a long time to build a positive culture, and it takes a lot of energy to sustain it. So a new entrant in an industry, seeking to build a competitive organization, had their work cut out for them. They could license the technology, build the production capability, create the distribution network, and rent the office space. But none of this would give them any sustainable competitive advantage unless they could also build a unique culture that integrated all of the pieces of this puzzle with a common logic that was near and dear to the hearts and minds of their people.

This is quite a challenge, because today, on a global scale, the cultural bandwidth to create an integrated organization is in scarce supply. This is partly because the skills necessary to integrate a global corporation are actually quite specific to that corporation. Sure, we always need to hire great talent from the outside, but organizations that aren't creating this capacity internally will always be at a disadvantage. This is especially true when a firm tries to make the transition from playing catch-up to becoming an industry leader with no one left to imitate except themselves.

This challenge is clearly greatest in emerging markets. The race is on. The struggle to win the war for talent and simply get the right person into the right job often leaves us exhausted at the end of the day. And there are still many more positions to fill! But the real target, as we enter this exciting new era of global competition, will always be to build exceptional organizational capabilities, on the ground, that build the firm's competitive advantage for the future.

7

BUILDING A GLOBAL BUSINESS *FROM* AN EMERGING MARKET

In the past decade, high-profile companies from emerging markets have surprised analysts by expanding dramatically in "mature" markets. They have expanded through organic growth and by acquiring companies in other emerging markets, but they have also expanded by acquiring established multinationals in developed markets. And the phenomenon is not linked to just one industry. The auto, computer, pharmaceutical, mining, and luxury goods industries have all seen companies from the emerging markets acquire companies in the developed markets. Examples include Lenovo's (China) purchase of IBM; AmBev's (Brazil) purchase of Interbrew (Belgium) to create InBev, which then bought Anheuser-Busch (USA); Mittal Steel's takeover of Arcelor to form ArcelorMittal; Lupin Pharmaceuticals's (India) acquisition of Hormosan Pharma (Germany); Yanzhou Coal Mining Company's (China) purchase of Felix Resources (Australia); and China Haidian Holdings's acquisition of the watchmaker Eterna (Switzerland). The list keeps growing.

The Boston Consulting Group (BCG) noticed this trend a few years ago and began publishing a list of "Global Challengers."[1] These organizations were the ones from the emerging economies that were the most successful at globalizing their businesses. The Global Challengers came primarily from the BRIC countries (Brazil, Russia, India, and China)—such as China State Construction, CHINT Group, Embraer, Marcopolo, Bharti Airtel, Lupin Pharmaceuticals, and Gazprom—and are now competing directly with established multinationals for global leadership in their industries.[2] But the number of companies from emerging markets that were expanding globally was growing so quickly that in 2011 BCG added a new category: Global Challenger Emeritus. This first group of Emeriti included Vale, the Brazilian mining company that is the focus of our discussion in this chapter. Vale was a Global Challenger in 2006, but now looks much more like an established multinational.

How do emerging market companies grow into Global Challengers? Research has shown that organizations in emerging markets pursue cross-border acquisitions to gain competencies such as technologies, assets, or brands. They typically do so by going through three stages: they start in their home countries, internationalize by expanding to similar markets nearby, and finally go global. During each stage they learn a set of lessons that can be applied to the next stage.[3] An essential part of this learning process is the adaptation of the organization's culture to a global environment and a global role. To succeed, they must learn as they go. They may have all the systems and processes in place to execute strategy, but if they are not quick to learn and adapt their culture, then they are unlikely to succeed.

The first stage of the adaptation process is a focus on getting the organization's house in order in their home market. Organizations must adapt internally to create a strong and unified culture that is the foundation for growth. In the second stage, organizations test the waters by expanding in the markets and products that are most similar to their home markets, diversifying through joint ventures, strategic alliances, or acquisitions. Again, these developments allow organizations to adapt their structures, cultures, and business practices to an international set of demands. Finally, to create a truly global reach, organizations typically push forward, with both organic growth strategies and growth through acquisitions, to establish a sustainable global footprint. To successfully navigate these three stages, organizations must closely align their cultural adaptation with their strategic objectives.

In this chapter, we will follow the development of Vale through these three stages. In 2001 they were a state-owned iron ore company that was hierarchical but decentralized. How is it possible to have a hierarchical, top-down culture in a decentralized company? In Vale's case, the company was organized around individual mines. The head of each mining operation had a clear mandate from headquarters regarding the results they were supposed to achieve, but how those leaders went about achieving their results was up to them. And the mines were usually a long way from the headquarters in Rio de Janeiro.

In the second stage of their evolution, Vale's focus shifted to becoming an international organization. During this time the pendulum started to swing toward the centralization and professionalization of the organization. Their managers started to benefit from a bit more freedom and autonomy. In the third stage, Vale grew into a well-established, highly professionalized global player with a more adaptable and open culture. This moved the pendulum back again toward decentralization and empowerment, but now with a much higher level of professionalism. By 2011 Vale had achieved outstanding business results that were acknowledged by their promotion to the Global Challengers "Emeritus" category.

Becoming a Global Challenger

It was in 1942 when the Brazilian government took control of two mining companies and a railway and created Vale's predecessor, Companhia Vale do Rio Doce (CVRD). (For simplicity's sake we refer to the company as Vale throughout the chapter, although it was known as CVRD until it adopted Vale as the global brand in 2007.) Over time it flourished and grew, adding both shipping and port management to its mining and railway operations. Its modern era began in 1997 when the Brazilian government began to privatize the iron ore company. Vale was fully privatized in March 2001, and in July of that year Roger Agnelli was appointed CEO. (In keeping with the Vale culture, we refer to Mr. Agnelli throughout the chapter as Roger.) According to company documents, his vision was for Vale "to become a global mining-focused multi-business company and a major global competitor in logistics and energy-related business, with a market valuation of $25 billion in 2010."

Getting the Brazilian Business in Order

When Roger took over as CEO, Vale was just starting to adjust to its status as a privately owned company. They still operated as a government-owned iron-ore company. During this period Vale described itself as "one of the world's largest producers and exporters of iron ore and pellets. We are the largest diversified mining company in the Americas by market capitalizations and one of the largest companies in Brazil."[4]

To become an international iron ore company and then a global mining company, Vale had to change both their mindset and their structure while simultaneously expanding their international operations. The biggest mindset change required was for its leaders to view Vale as one company. This was easier said than done. In 2001, Vale's culture was quite fragmented, made up of a series of mines that in most cases were run like individual fiefdoms. Each of Vale's business groups was run independently, and they did not use the same back-office operations. This resulted in a great variety of idiosyncrasies in the way in which the organization's back-office operations—finance, purchasing, logistics, accounting, human resources (HR), and operations—were organized. In addition, the decision-making process was informal. The CFO commented that in those days many of the relationships with suppliers were based on nothing more than a handshake. This made it very difficult for new managers to understand what kind of commitments Vale had made and how some of these relationships could be more formally structured. This gave Vale the unusual corporate culture mentioned earlier—informal, yet hierarchical and decentralized.

One of Roger's key priorities in these early days was to create "one Vale." This meant that the first step in the process was to move toward a more centralized model that would eliminate the individual fiefdoms that existed throughout the company. To do this, Vale started to standardize practices in human resources, finance, supply chain, accounting, and other processes. This included the introduction of standard ordering procedures, formalized contracting processes (rather than handshakes), consistent financial audits, regular performance appraisals, and much, much more. Getting the Brazilian business in order meant the introduction of professional standards in all functions and operations. These new standards helped diminish the power of the fiefdoms, as did the introduction of the same standard financial performance measures for all of the mining operations. This meant that the culture slowly shifted from local fiefdoms to a more professional mindset. At the same time, Roger refocused Vale's strategy on its mining, logistics, and energy businesses.

Although the professionalization of Vale was helped by the introduction of standardized processes, a professional mindset was more difficult to create. The legacy of having had a strong fiefdom culture in both the mines and headquarters meant that most people were passive—used to waiting to be told what to do and how to do it. There was also a culture of blame. Managers knew that when mistakes were made, someone had to pay the price rather than learning from the mistakes and trying to improve. For example, when a section of a primary rainforest was mistakenly logged, Vale fired the person responsible rather than trying to understand and correct the process that had led to the problem. So although professional processes and structures were introduced relatively easily, the mindset shift from passive to active and from blaming to learning took much longer.

Becoming an Internationally Diversified Company

By 2003, Vale had made a lot of progress in getting their house in order, At this point, they started to adjust their vision of the future and what it might be:

> To be a Brazilian global business company ranking [among] the world's three leading diversified mining companies, and to achieve excellence in research, development, project implementation and business operations by 2010.[5]

As Vale expanded into other countries—such as Australia, China, Indonesia, and Canada—they typically used Brazilians rather than locals for the key leadership positions, such as senior geologist and country manager, because they feared losing control or hiring someone who did not "know the Vale way of doing things." Sending out expatriates who were familiar with the informal, top-down, and centralized way of doing business was an important step in the process of combining professionalization and empowerment in their uniquely Brazilian way. Because they knew the "Vale way," these Brazilian expats were allowed to operate more independently.

But even when the top management team and the Brazilian expats had a well-defined and well-understood strategy, they did not always communicate it well to the rest of the organization. Their involvement of the middle managers in running the local businesses still had a long way to go. Corporate HR helped by working with the businesses to define the capabilities that they needed—immediate, medium-term and long-term—to deliver on the company strategy. Succession planning was one key area in which they made a major improvement.

Many leaders also noted that changing HR's interaction with the business was a fundamental step for Vale to create one culture and mindset and become a global mining company. They also involved the lower levels of management by launching

Vale's Corporate University, to provide technical, geological, and leadership training to all levels of management. This was essential in spreading the Vale culture and in driving Vale's transformation. The HR executive director noted:

> The first challenge was to determine if we were going to do a turnaround (change in a short period or time) or a transformation (making gradual changes with the people and assets available). I believed we were doing a transformation. So, we had to develop a people strategy because we did not have enough capabilities for sustained growth. We did this at the same time that we were transforming the Brazilian iron ore company into a global, diversified company.

The company also continued to create "one Vale" by creating a shared service department, which consolidated all back-office functions into one central operation. This included procurement, warehouse and inventory management, recruitment, payroll, training, execution, benefits administration, accounts payable, accounts receivable, and tax collection. In creating this department, Vale not only looked for synergies throughout the company but also captured and built upon their experience integrating earlier acquisitions. The director of the Shared Services group described their mission:

> The whole idea of implementing shared services was to create what we are calling a "plug and play" back office; that we can absorb or integrate a new company or even a project that is coming into operation into this Vale management model a lot faster than we did before.

To assess the progress they had made, in 2006 Vale asked its top two hundred leaders to complete our Organizational Culture Survey. As the results in Figure 7.1 show, the company had done

Figure 7.1. 2006 Culture Survey Results: Vale

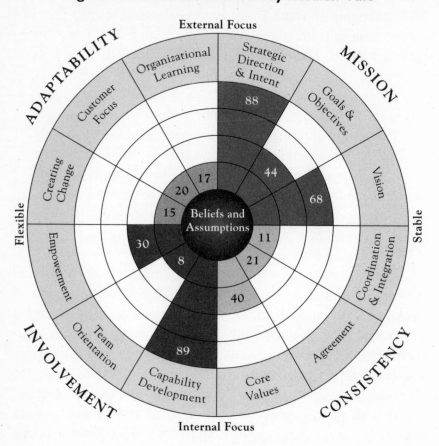

a great job in communicating the strategy and in developing its own people. However, the results show that the blame culture was still alive and well and that different business units did not work well together. In spite of taking many steps to internationalize, their scores on adaptability—creating change, customer focus, and organizational learning—were still very low. So although great progress had been made in terms of having one vision and strategy, there was still a silo mentality in the different local organizations.

Our Role at Vale

In 2005 Vale contacted us at IMD to create a leadership program for the top two hundred leaders in the organization. Because Vale was in the middle of a major culture shift, we agreed to do an organizational culture diagnostic to serve as a foundation for their leadership program. In addition to designing and delivering this leadership program, we then also facilitated a number of workshops, leadership forums, and executive board retreats. More recently we have also developed a more tailored talent management program for Vale at IMD. We also published an IMD teaching case on the culture change process at Vale.

Going Global

During this third stage, Vale became more serious about becoming a truly global, diversified mining company. They had to expand their product lines and their geographic reach. In August 2006, Vale made an all-cash offer for the Canadian nickel mining company Inco. This was the largest deal ever done in either Latin America or Canada, and it was bigger than the total of all of Vale's other acquisitions *combined*. The acquisition came as a surprise to both the industry and to Inco. As one Inco executive said, "Who were these people coming from Brazil? We had never heard of them."[6]

The cultural differences between Vale and Vale Inco were also apparent in the survey results (see Figure 7.2). Managers were not given much discretion in decision making, but the managers at Vale Inco in Canada were used to a decentralized organization, which gave them a much wider scope in which to achieve their goals. Their scores on empowerment, team orientation, and organizational learning were much higher than Vale's. However,

Figure 7.2. Comparing 2006 Culture Survey Results: Vale (Overall) Versus Inco

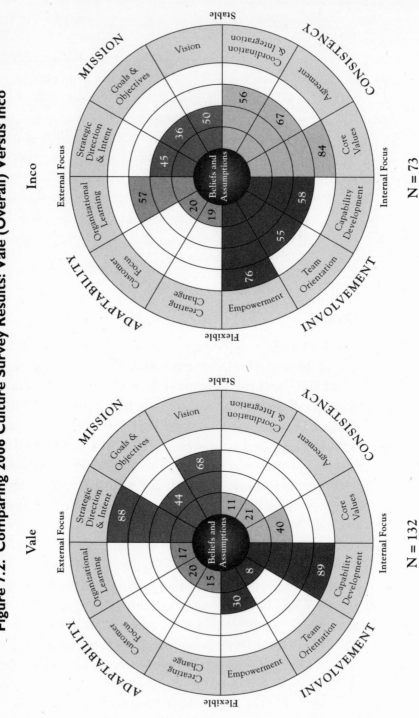

Source: Hooijberg and Lane, 2009.

Vale was much higher on strategic direction and intent, vision, and capability development.

The different national cultures also played an important part in the survey results. The managers in North America expected their leaders to explain why a process or system was being implemented and expected that they would be consulted about how the changes should be implemented. The Brazilian managers, coming from a more top-down culture, did not expect to be asked for so many explanations or consultations. As one leader described it, Inco's culture had always been one in which top management decided the general direction and then delegated the implementation to the middle managers, who were given the freedom and decision-making authority to achieve those goals. On the one hand, from the Inco perspective, Vale executives didn't always communicate the context for their decisions very clearly. For example, when they decided to create one global compensation system, Vale headquarters simply sent an e-mail instructing Inco to implement the new compensation plan, rather than going to Canada and explaining the logic behind the new plan. On the other hand, the Brazilians always thought that the Canadians were spending too much time questioning their decisions.

Communicating across cultures always has its challenges. One of the key lessons that the Canadians and the Brazilians learned while working together was about the way that they used the words "question" (*pergunta*) and "doubt" (*dúvida*). In Portuguese, the words are distinct, but the concepts are closely linked together. In Portuguese, you ask a *pergunta* because you have a *dúvida*. *Dúvida* does not imply a lack of trust or confidence in the same way that "doubt" does in English; it simply signals a gap in understanding, a challenge to be resolved, or an issue about which someone has a question.

So when Vale executives visited Inco, they expressed lots of *dúvidas*—issues about which they had questions. But they often used the English word "doubt" to describe the issues they were trying to understand. The Canadians often took this as a lack of confidence, or an absence of trust, rather than an expression of curiosity. That was not what the Brazilians intended, but it took everyone several months to realize the problems that this misunderstanding had created.

In 2007 Vale continued their global expansion by buying the Australian coal mining company AMCI Holdings. AMCI had been put together by private equity investors in the early 2000s with the goal of a quick sale. Because of this background, AMCI had minimal systems and processes; AMCI's managers found it relatively easy to implement Vale's "plug-and-play" shared services concept. The overall integration of AMCI into Vale had its challenges, but it was much smoother than the Vale Inco integration.

During this acquisition period Vale also decided to try to create more bottom-up participation. To achieve this goal, they created two executive programs to develop their senior leaders: in the United States MIT created a program for general management, and in Switzerland IMD developed a program for leadership training. These programs addressed multiple items that were identified by the Culture Survey. First, both programs were clearly focused on developing capability. Second, the programs directly addressed some of the challenges identified in areas such as empowerment, teamwork, organizational learning, creating change, agreement, and coordination.

The leadership program focused on such topics as organizational culture, change management, self-awareness, and working as a team. One of the key elements in the program was the use of a 360-degree feedback tool, based on the same model as the Culture Survey. In Vale, this was the first time that direct reports and peers, in addition to bosses, had provided feedback on the managers' leadership behaviors. This was a huge step in a traditionally top-down culture. The results of the Culture Survey itself were also openly discussed. Each program also included an executive director who held an open-ended discussion with the participants on the last day of the program.

Bottom-up participation was further encouraged in the Global Leadership Forums that Vale organized in 2007 and 2008, providing a chance for the top five hundred leaders to meet face-to-face and discuss the issues confronting the company. These forums provided top management with a way to deliver their views on Vale's future and an opportunity for the participants to air their opinions about the challenges they faced and how Vale's approach was working.

By 2009, Vale had become a diversified global mining company. Along with the changes in the business portfolio and the geography, the culture had also changed significantly. The results from the 2008 Culture Survey, shown in Figure 7.3, reveal that almost all areas saw significant improvements. The results were especially impressive in the areas of empowerment, core values, and vision. Another example of progress is that the culture profiles for Vale and Vale Inco, presented in Figure 7.4, now looked very similar, indicating that a relatively high level of integration had been achieved.

These improvements did not just show up in the survey results. We also saw these changes at the Global Leadership Forums and in the leadership courses. Employees sensed the difference. They felt that their opinions were taken into consideration and their voices were heard. One long-term employee noted that Vale's top leaders had become much more engaged and communicated better with their people. Another executive noted that the board was also more open to discussion, and that their openness and willingness to discuss cascaded down to the rest of Vale.

After 2006, Vale also began to hire more locals as senior managers or senior geologists, instead of relying only on Brazilian expatriates. The big advantage of this was that Vale could then learn from the local employees about their country's customs, traditions, and way of working. Many people remarked that the blame culture had changed: Vale made an effort to learn from mistakes rather than just looking for a scapegoat. However, they

Figure 7.3. 2008 Culture Survey Results: Vale

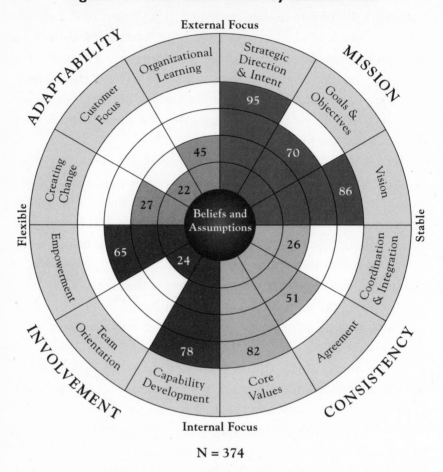

N = 374

also worried that the changed financial situation stemming from the 2008 financial crisis would bring back the blame culture.

The integration of Inco and AMCI Holdings also marked Vale's growing ability to manage using a global mindset. For example, when making decisions management would consider the impact on all its regions, not just the impact in Brazil. Vale also began attracting managers from the outside who embraced change; it was becoming a company with an increasingly younger mentality. The newer managers—in 2008, 70 percent of Vale managers had fewer than five years of experience with the

Figure 7.4. Comparing 2008 Culture Survey Results: Vale Versus Inco

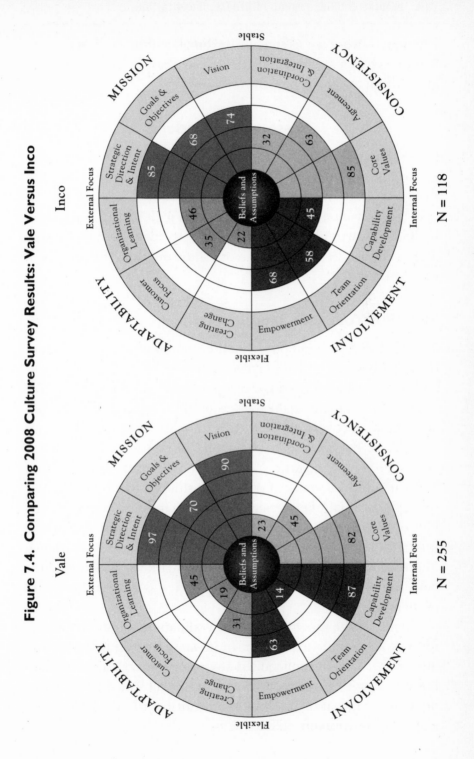

Vale

Inco

N = 255

N = 118

company—were not as steeped in the old culture and were more open to change. Overall, employees were more entrepreneurial and willing to try out new things.

Lessons for Leaders

In less than a decade, Vale transformed itself from a decentralized, government-owned organization with a top-down culture to one that was professional, centralized, empowered, and global. Its operating revenue grew from $3.1 billion in 2002 to $37.4 billion in 2008. Growth like this required Vale to adapt both its strategy and its culture. Several clear lessons stand out from this successful transformation.

First, Put Your Own House in Order

The 2011 BCG report noted that the emerging market companies that had become global players started by being "financially fit and able to take advantage of opportunities to buy attractive assets and compete against more established competitors that are still in recovery mode." As examples, they highlight not only Vale, but also such companies as Lenovo, Tata, Bharti Airtel, El Sewedy Electric, Yanzhou Coal Mining Company, and Wilmar International. All of these businesses first built up their strength nationally before aggressively expanding internationally. Not only were these companies financially fit before expanding internationally, but they also had acquired significant experience in integrating acquisitions in their local markets. This highlights both the professionalism of the companies as well as the clarity of their vision.

Many of the emerging market companies show similar patterns of geographic expansion. In its first one hundred years, up until 2000, Tata never acquired any companies outside of India's borders. Egypt's El Sewedy Electric was established in 1938 but didn't enter into its first joint venture until 2002 and didn't make its first acquisition until 2008.

The Balance Between Professionalism and Empowerment

Going global from an emerging market requires developing a culture of empowered professionals orchestrated by a centralized core. A lot of global expertise must be developed in the local markets to support successful decentralization, and a lot of local expertise must be developed in headquarters to support successful centralization. Organizations need to be both centralized and decentralized, according to what works best for thousands of processes and procedures. The right balance of professionalism and empowerment is hard to achieve—and harder to maintain.

As an example, at one point "professionalization" at Vale meant that the executive board became involved in the appointment of managers as many as four levels below the board. This standardization of procedures, KPIs, and appointment criteria allowed Vale to strongly influence the professionalization of its culture. The upgrade in professionalization also provided these companies with the trust in their leaders when they sent them abroad to run acquisitions, participate in partnerships, and build up greenfield sites. Centralizing the appointment of managers for a few years allowed the organization to then achieve greater decentralization of the operations as they developed more capability and trust on the ground.

Another interesting example of the importance of professionalism is Hindalco. In six years, Hindalco jumped from being India's largest producer of aluminum to being a major global player. They moved from supplying aluminum to others to acquiring the American company Novelis, a world leader in producing flat-rolled aluminum and aluminum products, for $6 billion in 2007. Another company Hindalco acquired along the way was Indal, an Indian manufacturer that not only developed aluminum products but also had developed the capacity to brand and distribute them.

But Indal's managers were worried that Hindalco's culture, which they characterized as a family business, would ruin their culture, which they viewed as professionally managed. Hindalco reassured them that it was buying talent, not just assets, and that they would always pick the best manager for the job. They backed up this claim by keeping Indal's senior management and giving the job of CFO of Hindalco after the merger to an Indal executive. Hindalco's integration consistently focused on using whichever business process works best.[7]

Building a Global Business from an Emerging Market: Beyond Vale

One of the most valuable lessons from Vale concerns the importance of vision. This theme is also strongly reflected in the experience of a number of the other Global Challengers. All of the examples we could find involved CEOs and other leaders with a remarkable sense of vision. At each stage, the vision was re-created to extend and energize these Global Challengers.

The importance of having a visionary, hard-driving CEO cannot be underestimated. Liu Chuanzhi, CEO of Lenovo during much of its history, began his journey soon after China took its first steps toward privatization. He had been employed by the Chinese Academy of Sciences (CAS) in its Institute of Computing Technology as a scientist and had participated in the development of over twenty mainframe computers. However, he was unhappy about the decline in the Computer Institute's prospects in the face of budget cuts and priorities shifting away from research on mainframes. When he decided to set up a company, funded with RMB 200,000, he and three others had to convince their scientific colleagues to overcome their distaste for business and join them in the unknown. They did not really have a plan other than wanting to take part in technology development. In the early days of the company, Liu insisted on maintaining close ties with the CAS. In 1985, one faction in Lenovo wanted to break free of the Academy. But Liu insisted that there were enormous advantages in maintaining the ties to the people, the research, and the financial backing.[8]

Liu went on to steer the organization through the changing Chinese landscape. He took control from the start in 1984 when the CAS funded Lenovo. He tried to make sure that the government had no say in the management—Lenovo had the right to control their finances, make hiring and firing decisions, and make decisions about the company's operations.[9] When the Chinese government refused to grant licenses to produce PCs on the mainland, Liu set up a factory in Hong Kong. When China entered into the WTO and Lenovo faced more international competition, he launched a series of mass-market PCs that were low-cost and high-quality.[10] Wong Mai Min, CFO and senior vice president, believes that Liu's visionary and strategic leadership contributed to Lenovo's success.[11]

It was not always a smooth ride for Lenovo. After Liu handed over management of the merged firm to Western managers, there was a culture clash that hampered its ability to strike a balance between IBM's focus on big customers and the faster-growing segments of the PC market for small businesses and customers. Furthermore, the 2008 financial crisis hit sales, and Lenovo experienced a $97 million loss in the quarter ending December 2008. Liu returned to manage the company. He was worried that the former CEO's management style was too top-down and dominant—with the CEO making the decision and then working with individual leaders of the top management team to implement it. This was in contrast to the consensus-based style Liu developed over the years "in which the CEO develops and implements strategy as part of a tight-knit group of executives."[12]

In the past, Westerners often thought of emerging economies primarily as a source of cheap production for the established economies. As this chapter demonstrates, however, it is clear that this view is way out of date. Global organizations need to recognize these as high-growth economies led by rapidly professionalizing companies with global aspirations.

8

BUILDING FOR THE FUTURE: TRADING OLD HABITS FOR NEW

All of the companies that we have studied in this book have viewed their organization's culture as a key part of their ability to compete as a business. Why do they see it that way? We believe they see that the culture reflects the core logic of the organization and the basic mindset of the people and helps define the firm's strategy for organizing. "The way we do things around here" is captured in the traditional habits and bundles of interconnected routines that define an organization's knowledge and capabilities. The culture is hard to understand from the outside and hard to change from the inside.

Many of the most popular definitions of organizational culture have emphasized three different levels of analysis: (1) the deep underlying beliefs and assumptions that are often difficult for insiders to articulate, (2) the values and principles that structure action, and (3) the symbols and artifacts that are visible on the surface for all to see.[1] This approach helps us to see that much of the knowledge we have as individuals and organizations is *tacit*—the knowledge is captured in our underlying beliefs and assumptions, and the knowledge informs our daily actions, but we aren't always very aware of how the two are linked. As in the iceberg we presented in Figure 1.1, most of the real substance lies under the surface.

"If only H-P knew what H-P knows," said the CEO of a major global consulting firm to us recently. The awareness of a firm's knowledge and how it gets applied is a major challenge in any organization. And it is closely related to the ability of the firm to compete. Consider Ratan Tata's commitment to developing a $2,500 car, the Tata Nano. Rather than viewing the project as an attempt to develop a dramatically less expensive car, Tata viewed their target customer as a family of four who are currently riding around on a motorbike. Tata's tacit knowledge of this market segment was a competitive advantage that no Western firm could ever duplicate. Their mindset was their advantage. The belief that the project was possible was their greatest asset.

Trading Old Habits for New

Although it has become popular to conceive of people and organizations as rational decision makers, it is also important to understand that a focus on key rituals, habits, and routines can explain a lot of what goes on in organizations on a day-to-day basis. This is also a powerful way to view culture for those who are trying to change organizations.[2] As psychologist William James noted many years ago, habit is the "flywheel" of society: "We must make automatic and habitual . . . as many useful actions as we can. The more of the details of our daily life we can hand over to the effortless custody of automation, the more our higher powers of mind will be set free for their proper work."[3]

When trying to lead culture change, it is always useful to view organizations as a bundle of interdependent rituals, habits, and routines. These routines capture knowledge and translate it into action in an efficient way that conserves energy and resources. The good news is that we don't have to think through everything that we do every time that we do it! But this also means that much of the essential logic of any organizational system tends to sink to an unconscious level, hidden from public view. This all tends to work fine until that moment when the world starts to change around us, and then we have to go through the difficult—and often expensive—process of rethinking what we do, how it fits together with the rest of the organization's capabilities, and how that creates value for the customers.

One of the best stories of innovation ever told is historian Elting Morrison's tale of the evolution of naval artillery, *Gunfire at Sea*.[4] Before the invention of continuous aim firing, cannons were solidly mounted to the side of a battleship. That made it very hard to aim! Continuous aim firing created a system in which the cannon moved back and forth with the motion of the waves so that a gunner could keep his aim on the target. The result? A 6,000-percent increase in accuracy. To understand the magnitude of this innovation, consider Morrison's account:

> In 1899 five ships of the North Atlantic Squadron fired five minutes each at a lightship hulk at the conventional range of 1600 yards. After twenty-five minutes of banging away, two hits had been made on the sails of the elderly vessel. Six years later one naval gunner made fifteen hits in one minute at a target 75 by 25 feet at the same range—1600 yards; half of them hit in a bull's eye 50 inches square. [p. 19]

So how long do you think it took for this unbelievable 6,000-percent improvement in accuracy to be translated into action and spread throughout the fleet? The real lesson from Morrison's story is that it took *over a generation* for this innovation to actually be adopted. Old habits die hard, and sometimes they die only with the people who hold them.

Morrison's essay opens with the story of a young time-and-motion expert trying to find a way to speed up artillery crews during World War I, just after the fall of France. He watched one of the five-man gun crews practicing in the field with their guns mounted on trailers, towed behind their trucks. Puzzled by certain aspects of their procedures, he took some slow-motion pictures of the soldiers performing the loading, aiming, and firing routines.

> When he ran these pictures over once or twice, he noticed something that appeared odd to him. A moment before the firing, two members of the gun crew ceased all activity and came to

attention for a three-second interval extending throughout the discharge of the gun. [p. 20]

Since this seemed like quite a waste of time, and the young time-and-motion expert really couldn't make any sense of it, he asked an old artillery colonel to look at the films to see if he could explain this strange behavior.

> The colonel, too, was puzzled. He asked to see the pictures again. "Ah," he said when the performance was over, "I have it. They are holding the horses." [p. 20]

A generation earlier, when the colonel fought in the Boer Wars in South Africa, it was important to "hold the horses." With horse-drawn artillery, if you didn't hold the horses, they would bolt, dragging the guns along with them. Bad scene. But now, with guns mounted on trailers that were towed by trucks, there was no more need to hold the horses. Nonetheless, the old habits die hard and the vestiges of the past tend to linger on, long after they have outlived their usefulness. The habits that were once an ingenious part of making a complex routine work effectively had become the "ritual inclusion of structure, that no longer serves any purpose."[5]

Habit is, to paraphrase Deepak Chopra, a frozen interpretation of the past that is used to plan the future.[6] An old Chinese proverb states that habits are "cobwebs at first, cables at last."[7] Warren Buffett described exactly the same dynamic when he said, "Bad habits are like chains that are too light to feel until they are too heavy to carry."[8] By the time we realize how restrictive our old habits have become, it is often too late to do very much about them.

Habits and routines are also difficult to change because they are so tightly interlinked. They fit together in complex chains of events that define "the way we do things around here." The cross-cultural classic *Kiss, Bow, or Shake Hands* shows how the most difficult aspect of executing routines correctly is that they require a shared mindset among multiple participants[9]. If you are trying to bow and the other party is trying to kiss, it really doesn't work very well. Changing only our own part of the equation seldom works, because all of the others are still linked together in the same way as before.

Suppose that an ambitious young chef decides to change the menu in his restaurant. Lots of other things must also change to support that decision: buying produce, training sous chefs, advertising, and explaining the new menu to waiters and waitresses all must change at the same time in a complementary fashion. A restaurant that we go to recently decided to change its menu to appeal more to "locavores"—those who favor eating foods that are locally grown. This not only makes a dramatic difference in how and where the restaurant buys its produce but also has a far more radical impact: The menu has to change continually in response to what is available, season by season, in the local region. As in many industrial companies, production, distribution, and the supply chain all have to change in a complementary way for the system to remain in harmony.

A Framework for Leading Culture Change

When talking about culture change, some authors have emphasized the importance of changing values,[10] whereas others have concentrated on the dynamics of the change process.[11] Still others advocate changing the business first and then making sure that the changes stick by institutionalizing the new way of working.[12] Others have worked hard to link the adaptation process to the mindset and underlying assumptions of the leaders.[13] All of these approaches are an essential part of any leader's toolkit and represent significant points of leverage that can be used to lead culture change.

But in our experience, making culture change stick requires digging a bit deeper into an organization's basic habits and routines. Routines link the abstract and concrete levels of culture in real time, and using that frame of reference for cultural transformation brings a vague cloud of opportunity down to earth in a rainstorm of practical action. Nonetheless, this emphasis on rituals, habits, and routines has received much less attention than the values and beliefs perspective, so we think that it is important to describe it here in some detail, as a way to summarize what we have learned from the research presented in this book.

To organize this, we have developed a simple framework to categorize rituals, habits, and routines that has been helpful to many organizations as they discuss their approach to transforming their cultures. One dimension of the framework contrasts the *old* with the *new*. Are the routines well grounded in the past traditions of the organization? Or are they newly constructed routines that have just recently been put in place? The other dimension of the framework is *good* versus *bad*. Are the routines effective or ineffective? Are they creating value? Or are they just the vestiges of the past that have outlived their usefulness? These four categories suggest four different types of action, as shown in Figure 8.1.

Bad Old Habits: Time to Unlearn and Leave Behind!

One of the strongest motivations for changing a culture is the dilemma posed by the set of bad old habits that have been around

Figure 8.1. Changing Culture by Changing Rituals, Habits, and Routines

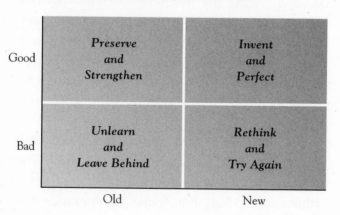

for years and have long outlived their usefulness. It can be hard to unlearn these well-established habits and leave them behind, but that's exactly what needs to happen. Let's consider three examples from the companies in this book.

The Old HR Process at Domino's. At the beginning of its transformation, Domino's had over a 150-percent annual turnover of people. The system of policies, practices, processes, and routines that created this situation had built up over the years as a reflection of a culture in which management almost always spent more time discussing the price of cheese than they did discussing the talent of their people. Their habits were very well-established. Individual store owners could do pretty much what they wanted, and typically they saw little connection between the quality of their people and the performance of their store. Corporate HQ generally kept their distance on this issue and at best offered guidelines for franchisees, rather than mandates for best practice. At the corporate level, there was also relatively little strategic HR planning or focus on capability development. Individual leaders came and went as they gained power or fell from favor. Little attention was paid to their development as leaders or to succession planning. All of these habits were well ingrained and had been in place for years.

The HR process was an easy target for improvement. It became very apparent, almost immediately, that this process was old and bad—and furthermore, that it clashed quite dramatically with the new CEO's values and approach to managing the organization. So it quickly popped up to the top of the chart of things to change, starting *now*. Once a leadership team or group of employees reaches consensus on a set of bad old habits to unlearn and leave behind, this helps to build dissatisfaction with the status quo and focus attention on alternatives for the future. This is one of the key strengths of identifying some of an organization's worst habits as a part of a target for change. It creates one more burning platform to help build momentum.

The Sales Process at DeutscheTech. In the year or two after merging adhesives, sealants, and surface treatments together into one business, DeutscheTech would still send two or three different salespeople out to visit customers representing these three different technology areas. They would compete for time on their customers' busy schedules. This set of habits not only created the impression that DeutscheTech was a collection of small vendors rather than one large vendor, but also created a barrier to the potential areas of collaboration between the related technology groups. The idea that the three different technologies could be combined in ways that would better address a customer's needs was at the core of the decision to merge the units. But in practice, it was very difficult to do until the sales process was integrated in a way that could actually deliver the integrated value to the customer. It was a classic example of how a decision to merge two units together may make perfect sense strategically but not be very visible to customers, because the habits and routines of the market-facing parts of the organization haven't yet been realigned with the strategy.

Both learning and unlearning were required to make this change stick. Individual salespeople needed to take a big step forward to learn how to actually sell the entire range of products in the newly combined adhesives business. On bigger projects, engineers also needed to unlearn the idea that they were the technical experts, able to answer all of the questions. They needed to learn to deliver as a team, in which they were the experts on the customer's needs, rather than about any specific part of the DeutscheTech technology. This example shows us one of the reasons that culture often takes so long to change. The culture reflects the logic by which knowledge gets translated into action. New knowledge, new people, new processes are all required to unlearn the bad old habits and leave them behind.

Fiefdoms at Vale. When Vale was first privatized, they had to confront the fact that the company was organized around individual mines. Traditionally, there was not much system-atic structure standing between the mines and the government bureaucracy. Plus, the mines were generally a long way from the headquarters in Rio. Because of that, the individual mines tended to be fiefdoms controlled by individual leaders. Finance, purchas-ing, logistics, accounting, human resources, and operations were all organized differently at each mine, with very little attention given to the operations of the corporation as a whole. They each had their own habits and routines, with little accountability. Little attention was paid to standardizing mine operations or coordinating capabilities among the mines.

The first steps in the process of creating "one Vale" focused on exactly this problem. Defining a new set of standardized business practices and processes to be adopted across the organization became the main thrust for getting the Brazilian business in order before taking the next steps toward globalization. At first this was unpopular and often viewed as disruptive. It generated a lot of resistance, even though it was absolutely essential if Vale were to move forward.

Every organization has a long list of bad old habits that they are trying to change. But just complaining about the bad habits and hoping that they will change is not nearly enough.[14] A clear focus on the areas of consensus about these targets for change can help to build progress and momentum and help develop the experience and conviction to take on bigger challenges.

Good Old Habits: Time to Preserve and Strengthen!

Sometimes, when organizations are undergoing widespread change, they can lose sight of some of the strengths that have made them great and end up "throwing the baby out with the bathwater." But some of the old and well-established habits and routines from an organization's past are still essential to the organization's success in the future. They are well understood by the people, they are a key part of the organization's mindset, and they are closely linked to other aspects of the organization's functioning. Therefore it is very important to clarify the core habits and routines that need to be preserved and strengthened. Here are three examples to help illustrate the importance of seeing the good old habits clearly.

Domino's Franchise Agreements: The OBI Clause. As we noted in Chapter Two, Domino's required all of their franchisees to sign an agreement that limited the franchisee's ability to maintain "outside business interests." This meant that all Domino's franchisees were completely focused on their pizza store. This legal requirement created a situation for each Domino's franchisee that was much like the situation for the first Domino's store, opened by founder Tom Monaghan and his brother Jim. Failure was not an option. And when success comes to that first store, what happens next? You open a second store! And then a third, and a fourth, and so on. This requirement created a singular focus that has helped build commitment throughout the Domino's system. Domino's choice to preserve and strengthen many of the time-tested practices and routines at the store level was an important part of their change strategy.

The OBI-related habits and routines also created some limitations for Domino's, especially as they expanded globally. It was impossible to maintain this focus as they developed relationships with master franchisees throughout the world, and they have sometimes had difficulties dealing with franchisees who had other options and interests. But overall, this principle was a tremendous strength that was preserved and strengthened as the Domino's transformation unfolded.

Polar Bank: Maintaining a Local Presence. One of the biggest challenges faced by Polar Bank was how to build a transnational European organization that could leverage the capabilities of their three different banking businesses across national boundaries. It was tempting, in that situation, to try to reallocate resources and attention away from the local businesses to help integrate the banks. But this was a risk that Polar Bank was reluctant to take. They saw that the strong local presence of the consumer banking business in Norway, the public finance business in Sweden, and the investment banking operations in Denmark was the foundation of the bank's future success, and they were reluctant to compromise that in any way.

The new capability of cross-border integration was a capability that needed to be built on the platform of a strong local presence in a way that did not compromise that strength. Thus it is a good example of choosing to preserve and strengthen a key orientation from the past, even as the bank built a new platform for the future.

GE Healthcare: Entrepreneurial Focus on the Value Segment. When GE Healthcare acquired Zymed in 2006 (and renamed it CSW), they instantly gained a strong position in the value-segment anesthesia business in China. Zymed posed several challenges for GE, but they also offered something unique—a Chinese-style family business with a strong sales focus and an entrepreneurial culture. They were thrifty, they executed extremely well, and they had a relentless and dynamic sales process. They also had deep roots in the Chinese market and its health care systems and needs.

But many of the entrepreneurial characteristics of Zymed presented challenges, because they were quite difficult to combine with the other two components of the organization, the higher-end Datex-Ohmeda anesthesia technology, and the process discipline of the GE global anesthesia business. But the D-O and GE perspectives brought little to the table in terms of tacit knowledge of the local market and the fast-moving, sales-oriented habits needed to capture market share in the dynamic Chinese market. As a consequence, GE redefined nearly every routine in the organization, and at each stage they had to weigh how they could apply the enormous technology and process expertise of D-O and GE, while still retaining the dynamic spirit of Zymed.

When the pace of change picks up, it can be easy to forget to protect those elements of the culture that made the organization great. If these factors aren't consciously protected from the beginning, they often disappear before you know it. And it is a lot harder to create them again the second time around.

Good New Habits: Time to Invent and Perfect!

Perhaps the most exciting part of the culture change process is the opportunity to create something new. Creating new routines to leverage new ideas in a new way can be the most exciting part of all. The canvas is not exactly blank, because the new routines must be well integrated with the other parts of the organization that do not change, but it is nonetheless a great opportunity to create something new. Again, we look at three examples of how some good new habits were created by our case study organizations.

Swiss Re Americas Division: Creating a New Operating Model. To implement a change from an old top-line strategy to a new bottom-line strategy, Swiss Re changed their operating model. What they really changed was the process by which they made decisions about their response to customer opportunities. Before the transformation, the client representative ruled. They would represent the client opportunity to the organization and work with the actuaries and underwriters internally to get a solution that would work for the client. They were less concerned about the profitability of the individual deal—and more concerned about growing top-line revenue.

The new operating model changed all that. Decisions about booking new business required a consensus among the client representative, the actuary, and the underwriter. It is a classic example of how a strategic change requires a change in a basic work routine and has a broad, practical impact on nearly everyone in an organization.

The Swiss Re case is also an interesting lesson in how important it is to find the pulse of an organization when you are trying to create a transformation. Their change to the new operating model took place during one of the busiest times of the year: the fall renewal season, when the organization was renewing contracts for the coming year. That's the heartbeat of the organization. During the busiest time of the year, they implemented the new operating model one week at a time, debriefing, learning, and strengthening as they went. At the end of that renewal cycle, they had implemented the new routine, implemented the new strategy, and created a new mindset among their people that supported this transformation.

Polar Bank: Creating a New System of Governance. To integrate three different banks in three different banking sectors in three different countries, Polar Bank chose to create one board that would govern all three banks. This bold change in the governance of the three banks created a totally new dynamic. Coordination started at the top, and the framework was set for cross-border learning. Standardization on the back office side, lessons about cross-border and cross-business marketing, and common approaches to managing risk and access to capital were all pursued by the same team, in the three different contexts. The creation of one board forced a level of integration that could have taken years to achieve if they had tried to achieve it at a lower level in the organization. The new board also combined the expertise in the three different banking sectors in a way that none of the individual banks could ever have done, creating a shared mindset that was the foundation for a full-service bank.

Polar Bank also invested quite a bit in a new system of leadership, whereby the leaders in each of the three banks were expected to develop expertise, understanding, and respect for all three of the banks, even though their specific job responsibilities were still squarely within one of the banking sectors. Some of them saw it as a waste of time, or an academic exercise that was "nice to have."

But others realized that any follow-up to the governance changes at the top depended on a cadre of leaders that were aligned with the new mindset that was taking shape at the top.

GE Healthcare China: A Vision-Led Integration. It was a bold step forward for Matti Lehtonen to decide that the integration of the strengths of Zymed, Datex-Ohmeda, and GE Clinical Systems Wuxi should be a "vision-led" integration. Why not process-led? Why not technology-led? Why not market-led? The choice of leading with vision raised a lot of questions at the time, but it did serve the purpose of defining a future state that built on the aspirations of each of the parts of the organization and that served as a platform for defining a common future working together. Once this common future vision was understood, that created a foundation for starting to integrate the three different parts of the organization.

Leading the process by defining a future vision had the interesting effect of creating a widespread consensus that new processes, routines, and habits would be created in almost every part of the organization, before actually defining what those processes were going to be. Most important, that allowed people to focus on the future that bound them together, rather than the diverse processes, values, and routines that could drive them apart. The discussion of "Whose process should we choose?" and "Which one of the three is right?" was deferred until everyone understood both the big picture and the strategic rationale behind the new organization.

Creating new rituals, habits, and routines is difficult. There are several pieces to the puzzle: Mindset, behavior, and systems must all change together to reinforce the adaptation process for the organization. As leaders, we can't just open up people's heads and rewire their brains, or prescribe a new set of behaviors that must be followed, or mandate a new system. We can't just grab one of those levers and start pulling. Instead, we need to gently but persistently push harder and harder on all three of those levers at once, until we see some of the signs of success that will encourage others to join in to help build the momentum.

Bad New Habits: Time to Rethink and Try Again!

Perhaps the most curious category of the four categories of habits and routines is the bad new habits that are sometimes created during culture change. Creating a new set of habits and routines doesn't always mean that they are going to work the way that they were intended the first time and that they will fit the situation well. On the contrary, culture change requires a lot of trial and error. In fact, the existing culture in every organization is made up of years of experimentation to find out what works the best and how that knowledge should be institutionalized. Thus these three examples drawn from our case studies point to situations in which the first attempt to create a new routine did not exactly hit the bull's-eye, but instead required some midcourse correction in order to get the job done.

Vale: The Centralized Approach to Integrating the Inco Acquisition. When Vale acquired the Canadian nickel producer Inco, it was the largest acquisition that had ever taken place in either Brazil or Canada. Vale's centralized approach to integration didn't give them the results that they wanted, so they were forced to rethink their approach and try again. Several expatriate assignments that sent Brazilians to Canada or sent Canadians to Rio didn't work out very well, and they were forced to try again. It took time to develop the alignment and control to be able to run this business effectively from headquarters.

Vale was quite adept at recognizing that they had missed the target and stepping back to refocus and try again. On the second round they were much more successful, both at running Inco on the ground in Canada and at representing Inco's interests well at the corporate level. It was their first experience at integrating a major acquisition, so the lessons of the initial phases of their integration process drove a rapid learning curve. With this experience, they did much better on their second attempt.

GT Automotive: Applying Service Learning Methods in the European Transformation. GT Automotive is an interesting example of how a culture change that was successful in one part of the world, North America, was extended to another part of the world, Europe. The interesting part is that most of the tactics employed to roll out this change process in North America were used as the foundation for the change process in Europe. There were some differences from one country to another, and certainly there was a different feel in the involvement meetings that took place in Italy from the ones that took place in Germany. But to our surprise, most of the process transferred quite well, with one exception: service learning.

Service learning involves organizational members in volunteer work or charity work in their communities. It has been used in many different settings to build a bond and a commitment within the team as they devote their time and effort to a community cause such as delivering meals, working at a homeless shelter, or helping underprivileged children. These efforts also show to themselves and to others that they are concerned with creating value beyond just increasing the profitability of their business. In North America, this was an important component of the change process in each of the locations. But in Europe, they discovered that this didn't have the same effect. So this key part of the change process was modified, on the fly, to maintain the momentum of the transformation.

GE: Improving Product Quality. Product quality with anesthesia equipment is serious business. When GE acquired Zymed, they experienced many quality problems. At one point, they even stopped production on the Zymed line until they were certain that they would be able to deliver high-quality machines that lived up to the GE reputation. Their attempt to resolve these problems required them to use a series of processes, each of which required a different set of routines and changes in mindset. At first, they simply needed to find and fix the quality problems as they arose. When customers had a complaint, GE engineers in

Wuxi would try to trace the model number back to the drawings that they had acquired from Zymed. But many times, those drawings weren't very accurate, or simply weren't available. Solving problems using this routine was very time-consuming and not very successful. Worse yet, it also took the engineering resources away from the product development process that would create the next generation of products.

To respond to quality problems, they had to get extremely good at find-and-fix routines. But to ensure that they had less to find and fix in the next production series, they also needed to introduce another new set of routines, borrowed from GE's legendary production process knowledge. They had difficulty adopting GE processes in total because, at least at first, they were unable to work to such a high standard. But they made steady progress in improving production quality and gradually created fewer find-and-fix problems for themselves.

But the third stage of evolution required them to improve their product quality by redesigning the product to eliminate even more of the quality concerns. This presented yet another set of routines to the GE engineering team. But even this redesign could not bring their quality to a level where they could seek FDA approval. That would come next, and it would present the team at Wuxi with the next set of challenging routines to master.

The culture of every organization represents the accumulated wisdom of years of experimentation. What works, sticks. What doesn't, doesn't. Just because an organization decides that it is going to change anew doesn't mean that it will get everything right the first time. Enlightened trial-and-error is especially important as we try to create the new rituals, habits, and routines that will transform an organization's culture.

Understanding the Importance of Routines

Think for a moment about all of the steps required to create that shiny new smartphone in your purse or pocket. Millions of separate events are integrated around the globe through a complex supply chain and a nearly endless set of business processes for design, production, and distribution. The human habits and routines that complement this highly technical process always reflect the core logic of how the organization operates. So it is important to see the close links between the mindset of the people, the systems that they have created, and their ability to survive in a competitive business world.

Routines and habits link knowledge to action. When we are trying to lead a cultural transformation, we have to rethink that connection. Connecting the visionary with the practical, the abstract with the concrete, and the principles with the practices is always at the core of any culture change.

Tracking Our Progress

Each of the case studies in this book was informed by an assessment of the culture of the organization at the beginning and the end of the story. The stories give us the clearest picture of what happened in each organization. But because it is sometimes hard to generalize about stories, the assessment was a useful way to track the cultural transformation. It also helped us pick a set of stories in which the positive changes in the survey results indicated that the organization was moving in the right direction. What's more, the assessment often informed the transformation process by forcing the organization to take a look in the mirror and understand their strengths and weaknesses more clearly. Of course, some parts of the culture can be accurately measured and tracked, whereas others cannot. Or, as Einstein had posted on his office wall at Princeton, "Not everything that counts can be counted, and not everything that can be counted, counts."

In addition to giving us a means to track the transformation process, the survey was also an intervention in its own right, designed to help drive the transformation. The results gave the members of the organization a good look at themselves. It was not always a pleasant experience. One president said, "It was like you told me that my baby was ugly. And smelled bad!" The results helped focus everyone's attention on the challenges that they faced. Groups, teams, departments, and divisions throughout these companies looked at the results and used them to plan how to improve.

Our role in these stories varied a lot. As we noted in each chapter, sometimes we were actively involved in planning and process consultation,[15] and in other cases we were teachers or organizational development consultants. We were connected with all of these organizations for at least two to three years, and we have worked with several of them for nearly a decade. Our involvement had a positive impact on all of these organizations, and we are proud of that.

But the most powerful catalysts for change in all of these organizations were the leaders themselves. The essential ingredient was always their insight, their vision, and their conviction that the time for change was *now*. They also had a lot of staying power. None of these organizations changed by making culture the flavor of the month. We learned a lot from them. This book is a way to share those important lessons with a broader audience, so that we don't all have to make all of these mistakes for ourselves.

Building for the Future

For nearly two decades, the top leaders of Japanese camera and copier giant Canon met each day at 7:00 A.M. for their Asakai morning meeting over tea. They typically spent about an hour together. There was no formal agenda. They talked about what they thought was important to talk about together. They talked about the principles and philosophies that they thought were most important for running their business. They talked about what was working and what was not. They talked about their people, their competitors, their products, and their technology. They listened a lot to their legendary leader, Fujio Mitarai, talk about the unique, evolving philosophy that had guided Canon through the years. But most of all, they talked about how it all fit together and what they wanted to create for the future at Canon. Their remarkable achievements stand clearly for all to see.

Very few organizations would ever take so much time at the top to ensure the alignment and integration of the leaders and their perspectives. But all global organizations that want to present one brand, one value proposition, one integrated set of products and services, and one team of talented and motivated individuals who are dedicated to their success need to find their own way of creating integrity. Different cultures and different industries may each have their own approach. Organizations old or new, large or small, may also have unique strengths that they can draw on. But in the end, to survive for the present and build for the future, leaders need to create a unique culture and mindset of their own, to differentiate themselves from the competition and gain the commitment and dedication of their people.

Appendix

DENISON ORGANIZATIONAL CULTURE SURVEY: OVERVIEW AND RESOURCE GUIDE

The Denison Organizational Culture Survey played an important role in all of the case studies presented in this book. The survey results were used in two very different ways. First, the survey results were used for *tracking* the progress of each firm as their story unfolded. This helped to substantiate our claim that these were companies that had made some real progress and also helped us to pinpoint some specific areas that showed more clearly the kind of progress they were making. In fact, several of the cases in the book were originally selected for this study because the positive changes in their survey results suggested that they had made a real transformation in both their organization and their business.

But the survey results were also used in a second way: as an *intervention*. The strengths and challenges defined by the survey results were used to drive the transformation process. The patterns identified by the survey helped focus attention on key priorities for change and helped guide the transformation process. The results served as a basis for feedback and action planning throughout the organization, so that managers could use the feedback to help plan the improvement process. Annual surveys over a period of several years also brought a new level of accountability to the ongoing change process.

This appendix provides a more detailed background on the survey and serves as a link to an extensive set of resources that back up the simple analyses that we present in each chapter. Here we address several key questions about the survey results, the benchmarking process, and the feedback and action planning process. We also present a description of the validation research and a summary of the research linking culture and performance that is the background for the model and the survey.

Interpreting the Survey Results

The core of the Denison Organizational Culture Survey is a sixty-item survey, with five questions about each of the twelve indexes in the model (Denison & Neale, 1996). The survey uses a five-point Likert scale, in which 1 = strongly disagree and 5 = strongly agree. This survey was developed out of the research done by Denison and his colleagues over the years, linking corporate culture and business performance. The model and the survey questions operationalize the characteristics of an effective organizational culture that were defined by the research. This research stream is summarized in greater detail later in this appendix.

The culture profiles presented in each of the chapters are simply an overview of the survey results. The more detailed results include a summary of the scores for all sixty items. Here we present a sample report and a brief example of how the survey was used in a real project. The seven-page sample report is presented in Figures A.1 through A.7. This example shows the profiles for two companies that have recently merged: a large American petrochemical company and the German specialty company it acquired. The acquiring company was about twenty times bigger than the acquisition, and the acquisition was folded into a division of the parent company that combined a set of closely related technologies to form a new global business unit.

This example presents detailed results for both companies and shows the contrast between the responses from the parent company and the acquisition. In the parent company, we surveyed all of the managers who were in the global business unit that absorbed this acquisition. In the acquisition, we surveyed all of the managers in the company. About 80 percent of the managers responded to the survey in each of the organizations. These data were collected just as the merger was approved and were presented to the transition team the very first time that they met together.

The overall profile on the first page of the report (Figure A.1) presents a classic picture, familiar to all of those who have pursued growth through acquisition. The dynamic, entrepreneurial, customer-focused acquisition is now a part of a much larger parent company that appears to be much less adaptive and flexible than the company that they acquired. The parent company paid top dollar for the acquisition. If the acquisition could influence the parent company to become more flexible, it would be a bargain. However, if the parent company makes the acquisition less adaptive, then it's not a very good deal. The results also show that both companies are fairly strong on involvement, but neither one has a very strong sense of mission. The results are mixed for both companies on consistency.

The more detailed results on pages two through seven of the report (Figures A.2 through A.7) show the picture more clearly. The "Gap Report" in Figure A.2 is a summary of the index scores presented in the profile in Figure A.1, showing clearly that the acquisition had stronger scores in ten out of twelve of the indexes, and that the acquisition had dramatically stronger scores in all areas of adaptability.

Page three of the report (Figure A.3) summarizes the results in the area of involvement. There are five items reported for each index. The scores for individual items, like the scores for the indexes, are presented as percentiles. The percentile scores indicate the percentage of firms in the benchmark database that scored lower than the target firm. So a percentile score of 82 for the parent company on the first item, "Most employees are highly involved in their work," means that the parent company scored higher than 82 percent of the firms in the benchmark database. The benchmark database, a large global sample of around a thousand firms, is described in greater detail later in this appendix.

Page three of the report also shows the contrasts between the two firms on each involvement item. For example, we have highlighted the item "Cooperation across different parts of the organization is actively encouraged." The big gap between these two scores shows a positive difference in favor of the parent company—it does appear that they put a lot of effort into and emphasis on coordination. The acquisition, dynamic as it is, operates as a fairly independent series of teams and departments that don't always emphasize cooperation.

Page four of the report (Figure A.4) summarizes the results for the consistency items. Here, for sake of illustration, we have highlighted two of the core values items: "Ignoring core values will get you in trouble" and "There is an ethical code that guides our behavior and tells us right from wrong." These items both show that the parent company has a far stronger set of core values than the acquisition. This worried the leaders of the acquired company, because they felt that the core values of the parent company were going to be imposed on them after the merger.

Page five of the report (Figure A.5) provides the results for adaptability, which show some of the biggest differences between the two companies. The first two items in the Creating Change index are highlighted to show some of the most extreme gaps in the areas of flexibility and the quality of the response to competitors. The five items in the second index, Customer Focus, also show big gaps across the board. In the third index we have also highlighted the item, "We view failure as an opportunity for learning and improvement," which shows a difference of 80 percentile points between the two companies!

Page six of the report (Figure A.6) shows the results for mission, which tends to show that there is plenty of room for improvement in both companies on this dimension. We've highlighted some of the results for strategic direction and intent and for long-term vision to show areas where both companies can use some help. The final page of this report (Figure A.7) simply summarizes the high and low scores for each of the organizations.

Figure A.I. Culture Survey Results for Parent and Acquisition Companies

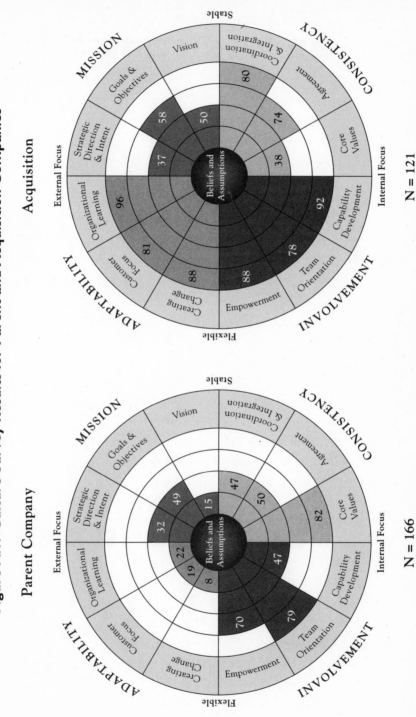

Source: Denison and Neale, 1996. Reprinted with permission. All rights reserved.

Figure A.2. Gap Report

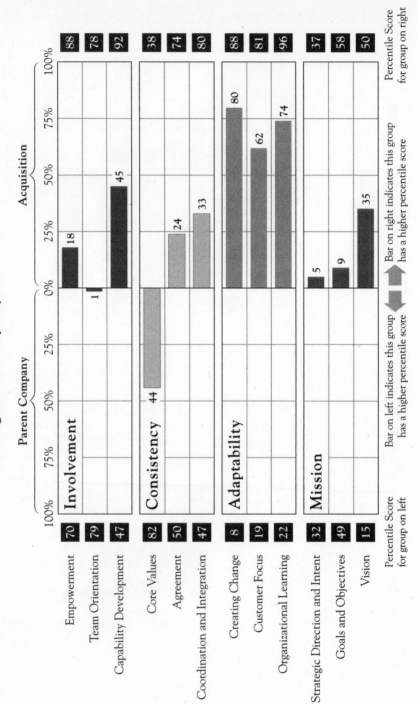

Figure A.3. Company Comparison for Involvement

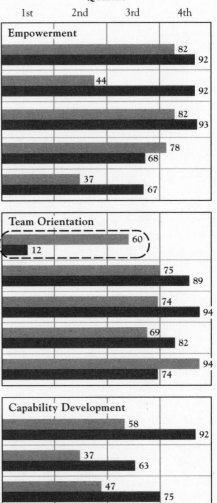

Involvement

Empowerment

In this organization . . .

Most employees are highly involved in their work. — Parent 82, Acquisition 92

Decisions are usually made at the level where the best information is available. — Parent 44, Acquisition 92

Information is widely shared so that everyone can get the information he or she needs when it's needed. — Parent 82, Acquisition 93

Everyone believes that he or she can have a positive impact. — Parent 78, Acquisition 68

Business planning is ongoing and involves everyone in the process to some degree. — Parent 37, Acquisition 67

Team Orientation

In this organization . . .

Cooperation across different parts of the organization is actively encouraged. — Parent 60, Acquisition 12

People work like they are part of a team. — Parent 75, Acquisition 89

Teamwork is used to get work done, rather than hierarchy. — Parent 74, Acquisition 94

Teams are our primary building blocks. — Parent 69, Acquisition 82

Work is organized so that each person can see the relationship between his or her job and the goals of the organization. — Parent 94, Acquisition 74

Capability Development

In this organization . . .

Authority is delegated so that people can act on their own. — Parent 58, Acquisition 92

The "bench strength" (capability of people) is constantly improving. — Parent 37, Acquisition 63

There is continuous investment in the skills of employees. — Parent 47, Acquisition 75

The capabilities of people are viewed as an important source of competitive advantage. — Parent 49, Acquisition 92

Problems often arise because we do not have the skills necessary to do the job.* — Parent 37, Acquisition 95

*The raw score has been reversed for this negatively worded item. In all cases, a higher score indicates a more favorable condition

Legend: Parent Company / Acquisition

Source: Denison and Neale, 1996. Reprinted with permission. All rights reserved.

Figure A.4. Company Comparison for Consistency

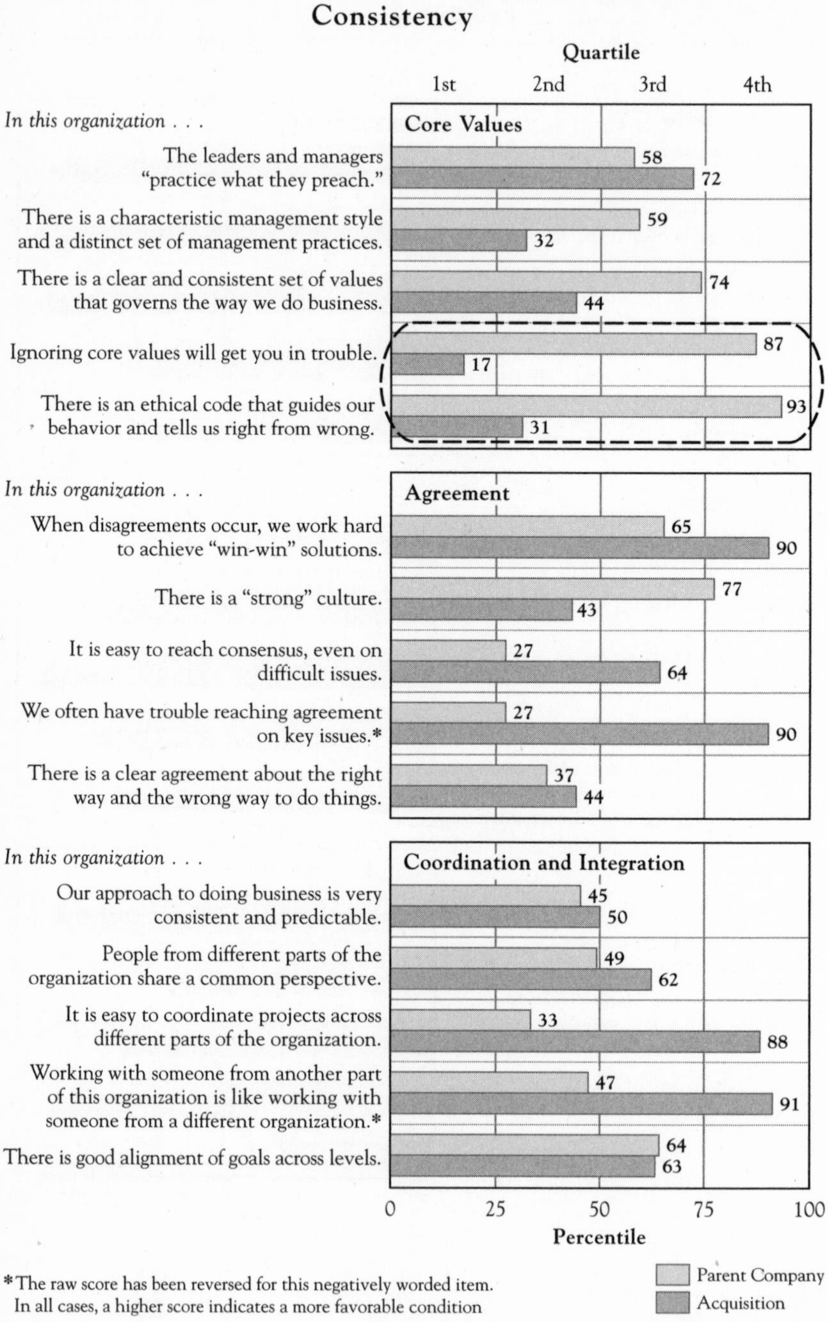

Consistency

In this organization . . .

Core Values

The leaders and managers "practice what they preach." — 58 / 72

There is a characteristic management style and a distinct set of management practices. — 59 / 32

There is a clear and consistent set of values that governs the way we do business. — 74 / 44

Ignoring core values will get you in trouble. — 87 / 17

There is an ethical code that guides our behavior and tells us right from wrong. — 93 / 31

In this organization . . .

Agreement

When disagreements occur, we work hard to achieve "win-win" solutions. — 65 / 90

There is a "strong" culture. — 77 / 43

It is easy to reach consensus, even on difficult issues. — 27 / 64

We often have trouble reaching agreement on key issues.* — 27 / 90

There is a clear agreement about the right way and the wrong way to do things. — 37 / 44

In this organization . . .

Coordination and Integration

Our approach to doing business is very consistent and predictable. — 45 / 50

People from different parts of the organization share a common perspective. — 49 / 62

It is easy to coordinate projects across different parts of the organization. — 33 / 88

Working with someone from another part of this organization is like working with someone from a different organization.* — 47 / 91

There is good alignment of goals across levels. — 64 / 63

*The raw score has been reversed for this negatively worded item.
In all cases, a higher score indicates a more favorable condition

Parent Company
Acquisition

Figure A.5. Company Comparison for Adaptability

Adaptability

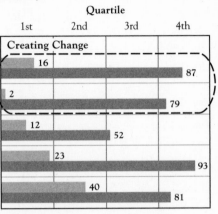

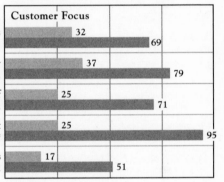
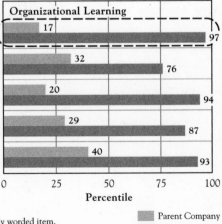

*The raw score has been reversed for this negatively worded item.
In all cases, a higher score indicates a more favorable condition

Parent Company
Acquisition

Source: Denison and Neale, 1996. Reprinted with permission. All rights reserved.

Figure A.6. Culture Survey Results for Mission

Mission

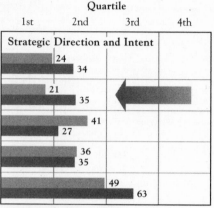

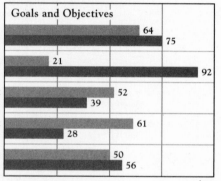

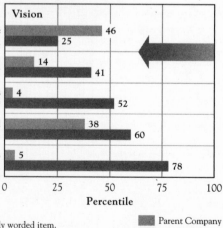

*The raw score has been reversed for this negatively worded item.
In all cases, a higher score indicates a more favorable condition

Parent Company
Acquisition

Source: Denison and Neale, 1996. Reprinted with permission. All rights reserved.

Figure A.7. Culture Survey Comparison: Highest and Lowest Scores

Parent Company

Highest Scores

94 Work is organized so that each person can see the relationship between his or her job and the goals of the organization.

93 There is an ethical code that guides our behavior and tells us right from wrong.

87 Ignoring core values will get you in trouble.

82 Most employees are highly involved in their work.

82 Information is widely shared so that everyone can get the information he or she needs when it's needed.

Lowest Scores

2 We respond well to competitors and other changes in the business environment.

4 Short-term thinking often compromises our long-term vision.*

5 We are able to meet short-term demands without compromising our long-term vision.

12 New and improved ways to do work are continually adopted.

14 Leaders have a long-term viewpoint.

Acquisition

Highest Scores

97 We view failure as an opportunity for learning and improvement.

95 Problems often arise because we do not have the skills necessary to do the job.*

95 The interests of the customer often get ignored in our decisions.*

94 Lots of things "fall between the cracks."*

94 Teamwork is used to get work done, rather than hierarchy.

Lowest Scores

12 Cooperation across different parts of the organization is actively encouraged.

17 Ignoring core values will get you in trouble.

25 We have a shared vision of what the organization will be like in the future.

27 There is a clear mission that gives meaning and direction to our work.

28 We continuously track our progress against our stated goals.

*The raw score has been reversed for this negatively worded item.
  In all cases, a higher score indicates a more favorable condition

Source: Denison and Neale, 1996. Reprinted with permission. All rights reserved.

All of the case studies in this organization have used detailed reports like this one for the organization as a whole and for the many different parts of the organization. For some organizations we produce literally hundreds of reports to help them understand the dynamics of different parts of the firm and to support a feedback and action planning process that addresses the needs of both the organization as a whole and the individual work groups within it. For more information on the survey and the different reporting formats, please visit our website, www.denisonconsulting.com.

Feedback and Action Planning

In each of the organizations discussed in this book, there was a substantial intervention that was designed to help turn the survey analysis into *action*. The most basic part of this effort was the feedback and action planning process that took place in each company. The people discussed the results in order to understand their meaning, see the pattern of strengths and weaknesses more clearly, and connect those results to opportunities for action.

This process usually started at the top, when we made a presentation of the results to the top management team. In most cases we presented the results, helped them interpret the patterns of strengths and challenges, and then facilitated a discussion that set some priorities for action for the team and the organization. The next step in the process was usually to move down the hierarchy with a feedback and action planning process at the division, region, country, function, or departmental level. Sometimes we did this ourselves, sometimes we worked with consultants, and sometimes we trained internal consultants who supported this part of the process. In some cases, especially after the first year of this process, the feedback and action planning process was largely led by the managers and executives themselves as they integrated this information into their regular management process.

Communication about the priorities for action was also a critical part of this process. Organizations that established a mechanism to share their priorities for change made the most progress. We even developed a web tool called the Action Planner for one client who was trying to summarize the priorities for action across hundreds of work groups around the world. The companies that got the most value from this also used the action planning process to share best practices for leading change across the organization, particularly when the feedback and action planning process included multiple units such as plants, stores, regions, countries, or departments that had different patterns of culture scores and different levels of performance. Discussions among the leaders of high- and low-performing parts of the organization almost always led to the sharing of good ideas.

Many companies also linked the feedback and action planning process to some aspect of their annual planning cycle and used the survey results to help guide their existing planning process. For example, one of the companies that we worked with held an annual "Strategy Week" for each of their four business units in June each year. The second year that they did the survey, they decided that they wanted to have all of the results ready for each of the business units so that it would inform their discussions during Strategy Week. Other companies always plan to have their results ready in September and October so that the results can support their planning process for the coming year.

Once the priorities for action are established, they can develop in a number of different directions. Some organizations need support in strategy development or strategy implementation, while others need a vision process or a balanced scorecard. Some need focus groups with their customers or some training in the process of leading change. Some need to create a network of cross-functional teams in product development, and others need to redefine their cultural brand to help with their recruiting. Some need help in organizing their supply chain, or in improving their quality, or in redefining their core values. This is just a short list of the types of things that often happen as companies begin focusing on their priorities for action. These priorities often imply that we need to bring in other forms of consulting support to help lead the changes that are required.

Many times, client organizations will ask us questions like "How do we improve our scores on customer focus?" The simple answer to this is that we don't have twelve silver bullets that we use to drive the improvement process. Why not? Because the solutions to a company's challenges are always very specific to their current situation. There are lots of great solutions looking for problems in the management literature. They are very powerful when used well in context, but they can be very destructive when applied across the board without much attention to the context. The questions that we always ask include: What's already being done? What's most common among the competitors you admire? What have you tried that didn't work? Where are the successes in this area that you need to expand? The key points of leverage to drive the change process become clear only when the context is well understood.

But even though each organization needs to find their own solutions to their own challenges, we have found that it does help if we can provide clients with lots of examples of how other companies have made improvements in their own organizations. Even though we don't recommend applying these suggestions directly without some serious thinking about how they fit, we do provide two summaries of the experiences of our clients in two documents on our website: "Pathways to Performance" and "Levers for Change."

The Benchmarking Process

Nearly all of the results that we present for the Culture Survey are presented in the form of percentiles. Why do we use percentiles? Because they allow us to present benchmarked results. Responses for all items are presented on a 100-point scale, and the benchmarking eliminates the noise of item-specific variation that often makes survey results so difficult to interpret.

Table A.1. Why We Use Percentiles

Survey Item	Mean Score	Percent Favorable (4s and 5s)	Percentile Score
Most employees are highly involved in their work.	3.94	86%	50
There is an ethical code that guides our behavior and tells us right from wrong.	3.78	82%	50
Customer input directly influences our decisions.	3.59	86%	50
People work like they are part of a team.	3.46	64%	50
There is good alignment of goals across levels.	3.21	57%	50
Our vision creates excitement and motivation for our employees.	3.04	41%	50
It is easy to coordinate across different parts of the organization.	2.81	40%	50

When we do workshops and training sessions, we use an exercise that is presented in Table A.1. When we first present the exercise, we only show the first two columns in the table: Mean Score for each of the items and Percent Favorable. We then ask the group to use that data to create a set of recommendations for the CEO of the organization. They are usually very creative and have lots of fun coming up with great ideas about how the people are probably highly engaged, but it will take greater vision and awareness of common purpose in order to build better coordination, and so on. Then we let the air out of the balloon, by showing them the last column that shows that each of these scores is exactly average—50th percentile. That's by design, since we picked the items in this exercise to reflect the 50th percentile for the highest and lowest mean scores with the items in the survey.

Then we ask a few simple questions: What would happen to the grand mean of the first item if it read "*All* employees are highly involved in their work" rather than "*Most* employees are highly involved in their work"? They quickly get this part right—the grand mean would go down, because using the word "all" rather than "most" sets a higher standard. How about the item with the lowest grand mean? "It is easy to coordinate across different parts of the organization." Using the word "easy" makes it very hard for respondents to give a highly favorable response to this item. So the mean score and the percent favorable response for this item tend to be lower, even though this mean score is still exactly the average.

When organizations use mean scores or percent favorable response scores to interpret results, their interpretation is heavily influenced by the way that the items are written. The items that set the lowest threshold get the most positive responses. The items that set the most difficult threshold get the least positive responses. Looking at items like this without benchmarks makes it very easy to identify the strengths and weaknesses of the organization based on the way that the survey items are written. That's bad news. Benchmarking eliminates this problem immediately. So we believe that it is important to use benchmarking whenever possible.

The most recent norms for the Culture Survey, created in 2011, are based on 931 organizations that were rated by over 465,000 total respondents. All organizations have taken the survey within the past ten years. On average, organizations included in the benchmark were rated by about five hundred employees. The number of respondents for each organization varies from as few as six respondents (in an organization with six people) to as many as 65,000 respondents. We include both small and large organizations in the benchmark because both small and large organizations will be compared to the benchmark. There are many important differences between small and large organizations, but there are not very many systematic differences in their survey scores. To calculate the overall benchmark, each individual organization is weighted equally. In other words, an organization that surveys three thousand people does not have a larger influence on the benchmark than an organization that surveys three hundred.

This benchmark database is updated every other year. For a detailed description of the benchmark database, please refer to the summary report on our website (Uehara & Denison, 2012).

Validation

The original development of the Culture Survey included several stages of refinement. Building on the earlier research by Denison (1984, 1990) and Denison and Mishra (1995), we developed a set of five items for each of the twelve indexes. Denison and Mishra (1995) provide the best account of the combination of qualitative and quantitative research that led to the development of the model itself. We went through several cycles of adding new items, collecting more data, testing the validity, and refining the measures. A series of working papers summarizes this research at several different stages of evolution. In general, our validation testing has always focused on the following set of priorities:

1. Confirming the internal consistency of the items in each index.

2. Establishing the discriminant validity that shows that items in one index are more closely related to the other items in the same index than they are to the items in other indexes.

3. The third stage of our validity testing is a bit more complicated. At this stage, we compare the "first order" and the "second order" model. This stage of the testing is designed to confirm that the "second order" model of sixty items, in twelve indexes, in four traits, fit the data better than just having one factor of sixty items, or four factors of fifteen items each.

4. After establishing the validity of the items at the individual level in steps 1, 2, and 3, we next addressed the internal

consistency of the responses for each organization. This is to confirm that the responses from an individual organization are reasonably consistent, in order to justify the aggregation of the results to the organization level.

5. The final part of the validation process is confirming that the survey results predict performance and support the core idea that there is a close link between the culture of the organization and the performance of the business. That research is summarized in greater detail in the research section of this appendix.

The validity testing that we've done over the years has generally shown positive results on all of these criteria of validity testing. A recent review article, which provides the best overall summary of the validation process, is available on our website (Denison, Nieminen, & Kotrba, in press). Other studies cited in the next section, summarizing the background research, also include a range of validation studies.

Research Overview

As we detailed in Chapter One, the Culture Survey and the conceptual model behind it were developed to operationalize a theory of cultural effectiveness that focused on the four key traits we have identified as drivers of organizational performance: involvement, consistency, adaptability, and mission. The traits were developed from a line of research by Denison and colleagues that combined qualitative and quantitative methods to examine the cultural characteristics of high- and low-performing organizations. This section gives a brief summary of that research and provides a number of citations.

The early research (Denison, 1982; 1984; 1990; Denison & Mishra, 1995) focused on the link between corporate culture and organizational effectiveness, and gradually developed the conceptual model as a way to frame the set of findings that emerged from the research about the culture characteristics of effective organizations. A second set of studies (Denison, Haaland, & Goelzer, 2003; Fey & Denison, 2003; Yilmaz & Ergun, 2008; Bonavia, Gasco, & Tomás, 2009; Denison, Xin, Guidroz, & Zhang, 2010) has a more global focus. This set of studies examines several global samples of firms and also includes specific studies that focus on Russia, Turkey, Spain, and China. A third stream of research includes more recent studies that further examine the link between organizational culture and business performance over time (Smerek & Denison, 2007; Gillespie, Denison, Haaland, Smerek, & Neale, 2008; Kotrba, Gillespie, Schmidt, Smerek, Ritchie, & Denison, 2012; Boyce, 2010). Finally, two recent reviews of the culture and performance literature by Sackmann (2011) and Denison, Nieminen, and Kotrba (in press) set this research in the broader stream of the organizational studies literature. Together, these studies help support the idea that the highest-performing organizations find ways to empower and engage their people (involvement), facilitate coordinated actions and promote the consistency of behaviors with core business values (consistency), translate the demands of the organizational environment into action (adaptability), and provide a clear sense of purpose and direction (mission).

The meaning and importance of similarly defined concepts have been described by a number of organizational scholars interested in the characteristics of high-performance organizations (Gordon & DiTomaso, 1992; Katz & Kahn, 1996/1978; Kotter & Heskett, 1992; Lawler, 1986; Martin, 1992; Mintzberg, 1989; Saffold, 1988; Schein, 2010; Selznick, 1957; Spreitzer, 1995, 1996). The culture model draws on contemporary theories of the dynamic tensions underlying organizational functioning and effectiveness (Denison, Hooijberg, & Quinn, 1995; Denison & Spreitzer, 1991; Quinn & Cameron, 1988) as well as classic approaches to studying the characteristics of effective social systems (Parsons, 1951; Katz & Kahn, 1966/1978; Lawrence &

Lorsch, 1967). These tensions reflect the fundamental pushes and pulls experienced by the organization as it tries to accomplish the twin goals of external adaptation and internal integration (Lawrence & Lorsch, 1967; Schein, 2010).

References

Bonavia, T., Gasco, V. J., & Tomás, D. B. (2009). Spanish adaptation and factor structure of the Denison Organizational Culture Survey. *Psicothema, 21*, 633–638.

Boyce, A. S. (2010). *Organizational climate and performance: An examination of causal priority*. (Doctoral dissertation, Michigan State University).

Denison, D. (1990). *Corporate culture and organizational effectiveness*. New York: Wiley.

Denison, D., Hooijberg, R., & Quinn, R. (1995). Paradox and performance: Toward a theory of behavioral complexity in managerial leadership. *Organization Science, 6*, 524–540.

Denison, D., & Mishra, A. (1995). Toward a theory of organizational culture and effectiveness. *Organizational Science, 6*, 204–223.

Denison, D. R. (1982). *The climate, culture, and effectiveness of work organizations: A study of organizational behavior and financial performance*. (Doctoral dissertation, University of Michigan).

Denison, D. R. (1984). Bringing corporate culture to the bottom line. *Organizational Dynamics, 13*, 4–22.

Denison, D. R., Haaland, S., & Goelzer, P. (2003). Corporate culture and organizational effectiveness: Is there a similar pattern around the world? *Advances in Global Leadership, 3*, 205–227.

Denison, D. R., & Neale, W. S. (1996). *Denison Organizational Culture Survey*. Ann Arbor, MI: Aviat.

Denison, D. R., Nieminen, L., & Kotrba, L. (in press). Diagnosing organizational cultures: A conceptual and empirical review of culture effectiveness surveys. *European Journal of Work and Organizational Psychology*.

Denison, D. R., & Spreitzer, G. (1991). Organizational culture and organizational development: A competing values approach. *Research in Organizational Change and Development, 5*, 1–21.

Denison, D. R., Xin, K., Guidroz, A. M., & Zhang, L. (2010). Corporate culture in Chinese organizations. In N. Ashkanasy, C. Wilderom, & M. Peterson (Eds.), *The handbook of organizational culture and climate* (2nd ed., pp. 561–581). Thousand Oaks, CA: SAGE.

Fey, C., & Denison, D. R. (2003). Organizational culture and effectiveness: Can an American theory be applied in Russia? *Organization Science, 14*, 686–706.

Gillespie, M., Denison, D. R., Haaland, S., Smerek, R., & Neale, W. (2008). Linking organizational culture and customer satisfaction: Results from two companies in different industries. *European Journal of Work and Organizational Psychology, 17*, 112–132.

Gordon, G., & DiTomaso, N. (1992). Predicting corporate performance from organizational culture. *Journal of Management Studies, 29*, 783–798.

Katz, D., & Kahn, R. (1966/1978). *The social psychology of organizations*. New York: Wiley.

Kotrba, L. M., Gillespie, M. A., Schmidt, A. M., Smerek, R. E., Ritchie, S. A., & Denison, D. R. (2012). The effects of cultural consistency on business performance. *Human Relations, 65*, 241–262.

Kotter, J., & Heskett, J. (1992). *Corporate culture and performance*. New York: Free Press.

Lawler, E. (1986). *High involvement management*. San Francisco: Jossey-Bass.

Lawrence, P., & Lorsch, J. (1967). *Organization and environment: Managing differentiation and integration*. Boston, MA: Harvard University Division of Research.

Martin, J. (1992). *Cultures in organizations: Three perspectives*. New York: Oxford University Press.

Mintzberg, H. (1989). *Mintzberg on management*. New York: Free Press.

Parsons, T. (1951). *The social system*. London: Routledge & Kegan Paul.

Quinn, R., & Cameron, K. (1988). *Paradox and transformation: Toward a theory of change in organization and management*. Cambridge, MA: Ballinger.

Sackmann, S. A. (2011). Culture and performance. In N. Ashkanasy, C. Wilderom, & M. Peterson (Eds.), *The handbook of organizational culture and climate* (2nd ed., pp. 188–224). Thousand Oaks, CA: SAGE.

Saffold, G. (1988). Culture traits, strength, and organizational performance: Moving beyond "strong" culture. *Academy of Management Review, 13*, 546–558.

Schein, E. (2010). *Organizational culture and leadership* (4th ed.). San Francisco: Jossey-Bass.

Selznick, P. (1957). *Leadership in administration*. Evanston, IL: Row & Peterson.

Smerek, R., & Denison, D. R. (2007). Social capital in organizations: Understanding the link to firm performance. *Academy of Management Best Paper Proceedings*.

Spreitzer, G. (1995). Psychological empowerment in the workplace: Dimensions, measurement, validation. *Academy of Management Journal, 38,* 1442–1466.

Spreitzer, G. (1996). Social structural characteristics of psychological empowerment. *Academy of Management Journal, 39,* 483–504.

Uehara, K., & Denison, D. R. (2012). *General report: 2011 DOCS norms.* Ann Arbor, MI: Denison Consulting.

Yilmaz, C., & Ergun, E. (2008). Organizational culture and firm effectiveness: An examination of relative effects of culture traits and the balanced culture hypothesis in an emerging economy. *Journal of World Business, 43*(3), 290–306.

Notes

Chapter One

1. Guerrera, Francesco. "Wells Fargo Cracks the Whip." *Financial Times*, August 24, 2008.
2. Gerstner, Louis V., Jr. *Who Says Elephants Can't Dance?* New York: HarperCollins, 2002.
3. Schneider, Benjamin. "The People Make the Place." *Personnel Psychology*, no. 40 (1987): 437–453.
4. Schein, Edgar H. *The Corporate Culture Survival Guide*. San Francisco: Jossey-Bass, 1999.
5. Acknowledgments for definitions: "The way we do things around here" from Peters, Thomas J., and Waterman, Robert H., Jr. *In Search of Excellence: Lessons from America's Best-Run Companies*. New York: Warner Books, 1982; "What we do when we think no one is looking" from Bryan Adkins, personal communication, 2008; "The code, the core logic, the software of the mind that organizes the behavior of the people" from Hofstede, Geert, and Hofstede, Gert Jan. *Cultures and Organizations: Software of the Mind*. New York: McGraw-Hill, 2005; "The lessons that we have learned that are important enough to pass on to the next generation" from Schein, Edgar H. *Organizational Culture and Leadership* (4th ed.). San Francisco: Jossey-Bass/Wiley, 2010.
6. Schein, *Organizational Culture and Leadership*.

7. Churchill, Winston. House of Commons (meeting in the House of Lords). October 28, 1943. http://www .winstonchurchill.org/learn/speeches/quotations

8. Rosenzweig, Phil. *The Halo Effect . . . and the Eight Other Business Delusions That Deceive Managers*. New York: Free Press, 2007.

9. Malinowski, Bronislaw. *Argonauts of the Western Pacific*. Prospect Heights, IL: Waveland Press, 1922.

10. Feynman, Richard. *Surely You're Joking, Mr. Feynman! (Adventures of a Curious Character)*. New York: Norton, 1985, 340.

11. See, for example, Lewis, Michael. *The Big Short*. New York: Norton, 2010; McLean, Bethany, and Nocera, Joe. *All the Devils Are Here*. New York: Penguin Press, 2010.

12. See Weeks, John. *Unpopular Culture. The Ritual of Complaint in a British Bank*. Chicago, IL: The University of Chicago Press, 2004, for an insightful analysis of how the ritual of complaint can become detached from reality.

13. Denison, Daniel R. *Corporate Culture and Organizational Effectiveness*. New York: Wiley, 1990. Our research linking culture and effectiveness is also summarized in the Appendix.

14. Denison, Daniel R., Hooijberg, Robert, & Quinn, Robert E. "Paradox and Performance: a Theory of Behavioral Complexity in Leadership." *Organizational Science* 6, no. 5 (1995): 524–540.

15. Lawrence, Paul R., and Lorsch, Jay W. *Organization and Environment*. Cambridge: Harvard University Press, 1967.

16. Fitzgerald, F. Scott. "The Crack Up," part one. *Esquire*, February 1936. http://www.esquire.com/features/the-crack-up

17. Kamprad, Ingvar. *A Furniture Dealer's Testament. A Little IKEA Dictionary*. Delft, Netherlands: Inter IKEA Systems B.V., 2007.

18. Ibid., p. 7.

19. Ibid., p. 14.

20. Jennings, Jason. *Less Is More: How Great Companies Use Productivity as a Competitive Tool in Business*. New York: Penguin Group, 2002, 16.
21. Schein, Edgar H. *The Corporate Culture Survival Guide*. San Francisco: Jossey-Bass, 1999.
22. Wingfield, Nick. "iPhone Software Sales Take Off: Apple's Jobs." *Wall Street Journal*, August 11, 2008, p.B1.
23. Krazit, Tom. "Apple Developers Mark a Year of iPhone Apps." *CNET News*, March 5, 2009. http://news.cnet.com
24. The principles of mass customization practiced by Ritz-Carlton can also be applied in the lower end of the market. The citizenM Hotel at Amsterdam's Schiphol Airport, for example, does mass customization for free. When you are in your room, you have lots of choices for ambience: lighting, music, temperature, alarms, and so on. Click once and you have saved those choices in your profile so they are waiting for you on your next visit. Not quite The Ritz, but it is a lot cheaper.
25. Liker, Jeffrey. *The Toyota Way*. New York: McGraw-Hill, 2004.
26. Ibid.
27. Rother, Mike, and Shook, John. *Learning to See: Value-Stream Mapping to Create Value and Eliminate MUDA*. Cambridge, MA: Lean Enterprise Institute, 2003.
28. Ohno, Taiichi. *Toyota Production System: Beyond Large-Scale Production*. Tokyo: Diamond, 1978.
29. Collins, Jim. *Good to Great: Why Some Companies Make the Leap . . . and Others Don't*. New York: HarperCollins, 2001.
30. Denison, Daniel R., and Uehara, Ken. "Denison Organizational Culture Survey: Overview of 2011 Normative Database." *Denison Consulting*, August 2011.
31. Kotter, John P. *Leading Change*. Boston: Harvard Business Press, 1996.
32. Charan, Ram. *Leadership in the Era of Economic Uncertainty: The New Rules for Getting the Right Things Done in Difficult Times*. New York: McGraw-Hill, 2008.

Chapter Two

1. Nonaka's writings on the Marines have never been published in English. This research is described briefly in his well-known book with Hiro Takeuchi, *The Knowledge Creating Company: How Japanese Companies Create the Dynamics of Innovation.* New York: Oxford University Press, 1995.
2. Bourdet, Dorothy. "Domino Effect: David Brandon Has Pizza Chain Shaking and Baking." *Detroit News*, December 9, 2006, p. 1.
3. Denison, Daniel R., and Lief, Colleen. "Domino's Pizza: Change Is Good." International Institute for Management Development, Lausanne, Switzerland, IMD 3–1839, 2008.
4. Ibid.
5. See the Appendix for an overview of the Survey results.
6. Denison and Lief, "Domino's Pizza, " p. 7.
7. The *spoodle* is a unique combination of a spoon and a ladle, with a measuring cup on one side that ensures that you have exactly the right amount of sauce for a pizza, and a flat surface on the other side for spreading the sauce.
8. Bartlett, Christopher, and Ghoshal, Sumantra. "Building Competitive Advantage Through People." *Sloan Management Review*, January 2002, 34–41.
9. McGregor, Douglas. *The Human Side of Enterprise*. New York: McGraw-Hill, 1960.
10. Likert, Rensis. *New Patterns of Management*. New York: McGraw-Hill, 1961.
11. Lawler, Edward E., III. *High-Involvement Management*. San Francisco: Jossey-Bass, 1986.
12. Kotter, *Leading Change* (see ch. 1, n. 31).
13. Collins, *Good to Great* (see ch. 1, n. 28).
14. Boudreau, John W., and Ramstad, Peter M. *Beyond HR: The New Science of Human Capital*. Boston: Harvard Business School Publishing, 2007; Likert, Rensis. *New Patterns of Management*. New York: McGraw-Hill, 1961.

15. Ibid., p. 54.
16. Davenport, Thomas H. "Competing on Analytics." *Harvard Business Review*, January 2006, 2–11.
17. Lawler, Edward E., III. *High-Involvement Management*. San Francisco: Jossey-Bass, 1991.
18. Katzenbach, Jon R., and Santamaria, Jason A. "Firing Up the Front Line." *Harvard Business Review*, May-June 1999, 1–12.

Chapter Three

1. Porter, Michael. "What Is Strategy?" *Harvard Business Review*, November-December 1996, 61–78.
2. Charan, Ram. *Leadership in the Era of Economic Uncertainty* (see ch. 1, n. 32).
3. Kaplan, Robert S., and Norton, David P. "Mastering the Management System." *Harvard Business Review*, January 2008, 63–77.
4. At the company's request, we have adopted a pseudonym for this firm.
5. Although statement 3 is negatively worded, its response scores are reversed(R), so a higher percentile score indicates a better condition for all five statements.
6. Denison, Daniel R. "Swiss Re Americas Division." Lausanne, Switzerland: IMD Business School, IMD 4–0281, 2004.
7. Nonaka, Ikujiro. "Toward Middle-Up-Down Management: Accelerating Information Creation." *Sloan Management Review* 29, no. 3 (1988): 9–18.
8. Covey, Stephen M. R. *The Speed of Trust: The One Thing That Changes Everything*. New York: Free Press, 2006.
9. Kaplan and Norton, "Mastering the Management System."
10. Two useful articles that give an overview of the alignment process are Collins, Jim, "Aligning with Vision and Values." *Leadership Excellence*, 23, no. 4 (2006): 6; Sull, Donald, "Closing the Gap Between Strategy and Execution." *MIT Sloan Management Review* 48, no. 4 (Summer 2007): 30–38.

11. Dresner, Howard. "Building a Performance-Directed Culture." *Balanced Scorecard Report* (Harvard Business Publishing), January-February 2010, 3–8.
12. Carr, Patricia. "Riding the Tiger of Culture Change." *T+D*, August 2004, 32–41.

Chapter Four

1. Yip, George, and Bink, Audrey J. M. *Managing Global Customers: An Integrated Approach*. New York: Oxford University Press, 2007.
2. Denison, Daniel R., Adkins, Bryan, and Guidroz, Ashley M. "Managing Cultural Integration in Cross-Border Mergers and Acquisitions." In *Advances in Global Leadership*, edited by William H. Mobley, Ming Li, and Ying Wang, vol. 6, 95–115. Bingley, UK: Emerald Group Publishing, 2011.
3. Marks, Mitchell Lee, and Mirvis, Philip H. *Joining Forces: Making One Plus One Equal Three in Mergers, Acquisitions, and Alliances*. San Francisco: Jossey-Bass, 2010, p. 4; Mirvis, Philip H., and Marks, Mitchell Lee. *Managing the Merger: Making It Work*. Upper Saddle River, NJ: Prentice Hall Professional Technical Reference, 1991.
4. Schraeder, Mike, and Self, Dennis R. "Enhancing the Success of Mergers and Acquisitions: An Organizational Culture Perspective." *Management Decision* 41, no. 5 (2003): 511.
5. At the company's request, we use a pseudonym for this financial services firm.
6. Collins, James C. *Good to Great: Why Some Companies Make the Leap—and Others Don't*. New York: HarperBusiness, 2001.
7. Marks and Mirvis, *Joining Forces*.
8. Moulton Reger, Sara J. *Can Two Rights Make a Wrong? Insights from IBM's Tangible Culture Approach*. Upper Saddle River, NJ: Pearson Education, 2006.

Chapter Five

1. Kriegel, Robert, and Brandt, David. *Sacred Cows Make the Best Burgers: Developing Change-Driving People and Organizations*. New York: Warner Books, 1996.

2. At the company's request, we have adopted a pseudonym for this firm.

3. Denison, Daniel R., and Lief, Colleen. "GT Automotive (A): Transforming a Corporate Culture." Lausanne, Switzerland: IMD Business School, IMD-4-0308, 2009; Denison, Daniel R., and Lief, Colleen. "GT Automotive (B): Building a Global Team." Lausanne, Switzerland: IMD Business School, IMD-4-0309, 2009.

4. Hofstede, Geert. *Culture's Consequences: Comparing Values, Behaviors, Institutions and Organizations Across Nations*. Thousand Oaks, CA: SAGE, 2001. See also Wilkins, Alan, and Ouchi, William. "Efficient Cultures: Exploring the Relationship Between Culture and Organizational Performance." *Administrative Science Quarterly* 28, no. 3 (1983): 468–481.

5. Gomez-Mejia, Luis R., and Palich, Leslie. "Cultural Diversity and the Performance of Multinational Firms." *Journal of International Business Studies* 28, no. 2 (1997): 309–335.

6. For years, our research team has studied the differences in our culture data from around the world. The shocking finding is that the differences are actually very small. In the Appendix to this book, you will find a more detailed description of these research studies.

7. Apfelthaler, Gerhard, Muller, Helen J., and Rehder, Robert R. "Corporate Culture as Competitive Advantage: Learning from Germany and Japan in Alabama and Austria?" *Journal of World Business* 37, no. 2 (2002): 108–118. See also Brock, David M., Barry, David, and Thomas, David C. "'Your Forward Is Our Reverse, Your Right, Our Wrong': Rethinking

Multinational Planning Processes in Light of National Culture." *International Business Review* 9, no. 6 (2000): 687–701.

8. Schneider, Susan, and Barsoux, Jean-Louis. *Managing Across Cultures*. Harlow, UK: Financial Times/Prentice Hall, 2003.

9. Weick, Karl. *Making Sense of the Organization*. Oxford, UK: Blackwell Publishing, 2001.

Chapter Six

1. Gifford, Rob. "China Leads World in High-Speed Rail Tracks." National Public Radio. November 16, 2010. http://www.npr.org/2010/11/16/131351045/china-leads-other-nations-in-high-speed-rail-tracks

2. Barboza, David. "G.M., Eclipsed at Home, Soars to Top in China." *New York Times*. July 21, 2010. http://www.nytimes.com/2010/07/22/business/global/22auto.html

3. Denison, Daniel R., Xin, Katherine, and Zhang, Lily. "GE Healthcare Life Support Solutions (A): Entering a New Global Market." Lausanne, Switzerland: IMD Business School, IMD-3–2074, 2009; Denison, Daniel R., Xin, Katherine, and Zhang, Lily. "GE Healthcare Life Support Solutions (B): A Vision-Led Integration." Lausanne, Switzerland: IMD Business School, IMD-3–2075, 2009; Denison, Daniel R., Xin, Katherine, and Zhang, Lily. "GE Healthcare Life Support Solutions (C): Positioning for Quality and Growth." Lausanne, Switzerland: IMD Business School, IMD-3–2076, 2009.

4. As noted earlier, when GE acquired this company it was named Zymed. After the acquisition, they created the name CSW (Clinical Systems Wuxi) to refer to the combination of Datex-Ohmeda (D-O) and Zymed.

5. Dunning, John H. *Multinational Enterprises and the Global Economy*. Workingham, UK: Addison-Wesley, 1992.

6. Barney, Jay. "Firm Resources and Sustained Competitive Advantage." *Journal of Management* 17, no. 1(1991): 99–120.

Chapter Seven

1. Aguiar, Marcos, et al. "The New Global Challengers: How 100 Top Companies from Rapidly Developing Economies Are Changing the World." Boston Consulting Group, May 2006.
2. Verma, Sharad, et al. "Companies on the Move: Rising Stars from Rapidly Developing Economies Are Reshaping Global Industries." Boston Consulting Group, January 2011.
3. Kumar, Nurmalia. "How Emerging Giants Are Rewriting the Rules of M&A." *Harvard Business Review* 87, no. 5 (2009): 115–121.
4. SEC Form 20F, 2002, retrieved from www.vale.com
5. Hooijberg, Robert, and Lane, Nancy. "Vale: Going Global (A)." International Institute for Management Development, Lausanne, Switzerland: IMD Business School, IMD-4-0312, 2009.
6. From an interview at the Global Leadership Forum, October 2008.
7. Kumar, "How Emerging Giants Are Rewriting the Rules of M&A."
8. Ling, Zhijun, and Avery, Martha. *The Lenovo Affair: The Growth of China's Computer Giant and Its Takeover of IBM-PC*. Singapore: Wiley Asia, 2006.
9. Ibid.
10. Schuman, Michael. "Lenovo's Legend Returns." *Time* 175, no. 18 (May 10, 2010): 1–7.
11. Millman, Gregory J. "From East to West." *Financial Executive* 24, no. 10 (December 2008): 31–33.
12. Schuman, "Lenovo's Legend Returns."

Chapter Eight

1. Schein, Edgar H. *Organizational Culture and Leadership* (3rd ed.). San Francisco: Jossey-Bass/Wiley, 2004.
2. Cohen, Michael D., and Bacdayan, Paul. "Organizational Routines Are Stored as Procedural Memory: Evidence from

a Laboratory Study." *Organization Science* 5, no. 4 (1994): 554–568; Cohen, Michael D. "Reading Dewey: Reflections on the Study of Routine." *Organization Studies* 28, no. 28 (2007): 773–786.

3. James, William. *The Principles of Psychology*. Cambridge, MA: Harvard University Press, 1890.

4. Morrison, Elting E. *Men, Machines, and Modern Times*. Cambridge, MA: MIT Press, 1966, 17–44.

5. Feynman, Richard. *Surely You're Joking, Mr. Feynman! (Adventures of a Curious Character)*. New York: Norton, 1985, 340.

6. Chopra's original quote is "A habit is a frozen interpretation from the past that is applied to the present." http://davesdailyquotes.com/?p=7594

7. See Stone, John R. *The Routledge Book of World Proverbs*. New York: Routledge, 2006, 199.

8. Clark, David. *The Tao of Warren Buffett: Warren Buffett's Words of Wisdom: Quotations and Interpretations to Help Guide You to Billionaire Wealth and Enlightened Business Management*. New York: Scribner, 2006, p. 16.

9. Conaway, Wayne A. *Kiss, Bow, or Shake Hands*. Avon, MA: F+W Media, 2006.

10. Lencioni, Patrick M. "Make Your Values Mean Something." *Harvard Business Review*, July 2002, 5.

11. Collins, Jim. *Good to Great: Why Some Companies Make the Leap . . . and Others Don't*. New York: HarperCollins, 2001.

12. Kotter, John P. *Leading Change*. Cambridge, MA: Harvard Business School Press, 1996.

13. Schein, Edgar H. *The Corporate Culture Survival Guide*. San Francisco: Jossey-Bass, 1999.

14. Weeks, John. *Unpopular Culture: The Ritual of Complaint in a British Bank*. Chicago: University of Chicago Press, 2004.

15. Schein, Edgar H. *Process Consultation: Its Role in Organization Development*, vol. 1. Boston: Addison-Wesley, 1969.

Acknowledgments

There are so many people who deserve our thanks for their contributions to this book, that it's hard to know where to start. I have been fortunate throughout my career to have so many positive influences on my work. It is hard to know where to begin. So I will try to do this chronologically and by institution in an effort not to leave anyone out. My apologies in advance for anyone I missed!

I want to start with a touch of "ancestor worship." My career really started when I joined the staff at the University of Michigan's Institute for Social Research. I was fortunate to work with several of the real pioneers in the field, including Rensis Likert, Jane Gibson Likert, Robert Kahn, Stanley Seashore, and David Bowers. When I moved to the Michigan Business School in 1987, my good fortune and rapid learning curve continued through my contact with Karl Weick, C. K. Prahalad, Kim Cameron, Bob Quinn, Stu Hart, Jane Dutton, Lance Sandelands, Jim Walsh, Sue Ashford, Jerry Davis, and Gerry Ross.

I left the University of Michigan in 1999 because it was clear that the next stage in my career would require a global perspective. Our family spent a wonderful sabbatical year at Hitotsubashi University in Tokyo in 1995–1996, where I fell under the influence of Ikujiro Nonaka and his colleagues Hiro Takeuchi, Sei Yonekura, and Kazuo Ichijo. Nonaka-Sensei's insights were still top-of-mind when I started writing this book fifteen years later. Just as we were leaving Japan, Vlado Pucik convinced me that I should come to Switzerland to visit the International Institute for Management Development (IMD) in Lausanne. IMD has now been my academic home for over twelve years, and it has been a dynamic and exciting place to work. During their tenures as president, Peter Lorange and Dominique Turpin have both been very generous and supportive of my work. The staff at IMD also help to make it a great place to work. Special thanks are due to Rahel Albrecht and Sophie Pedgrift as well as Cedric Vaucher, Petri Lehtivaara, Persita Egli, and the entire research and case-writing team.

But my most sincere thanks go to all my faculty colleagues at IMD. They are a constant source of fun and friendship and more new ideas than I can ever keep in my head at the same time. Special thanks are due to Shlomo Ben-Hur, Rolf Boscheck, Cyril Bouquet, Bettina Buchel, Bala Chakravarthy, Joe DiStefano, Albrecht Enders, Bill Fischer, Peter Killing, George Kohlrieser, Tom Malnight, Jean-Francois Manzoni, Martha Maznevski, Anand Narasimhan, Maury Peiperl, Phil Rosenzweig, Michael Watkins, and John Weeks.

My colleagues in the field of organizational studies have also been a great source of inspiration. I am most indebted to culture guru Edgar Schein for all of his gracious support and unending insights. One of the biggest delights of my career has been the interest that he has taken in this book. My IMD colleague John Weeks also earned my gratitude many times over for his thorough and insightful review of the first draft of this book. His comments guided my final revision of the manuscript in the last few weeks before the deadline.

There are many other colleagues in the field whom I would also like to thank: Ben Schneider, John VanMaanen, Ed Lawler, Mike Beer, John Kotter, Neal Ashkanasy, Susan Jackson, Bob Sutton, Steve Barley, Stew Friedman, Richard Hackman, Paul Lawrence, Geert Hofstede, Chris Argyris, Sonja Sackmann, Terry

Beehr, Chad Hartnell, Mark Ehrhart, Dave Hogberg, Robert Cooper, Dave Schwandt, Lou Tornatzky, Margaret Gorman, Mike Rother, Vic Strecher, Jeff Liker, Paula Caproni, Neil Sendelbach, and Michael McGrath. And that is just the start.

My colleagues at Denison Consulting in Ann Arbor, Michigan, also deserve my rich thanks and appreciation for all that they have contributed to this work. Bill Neale, Bryan Adkins, Jay Richards, Mark Simonson, Alice Wastag, Nabil Sousou, and Tim Kuppler have all supported this work in more ways than I can count. The R&D Team at DC is one of my proudest achievements and just keeps getting better all the time. Lindsey Kotrba, Levi Neiminen, Ken Uehara, Ia Ko, Ryan Smerek, and Ashley Guidroz have all made important contributions to this work. I couldn't have done it without their support. Jaren Hart provided great support to help me keep track of all of the rounds of "final" revisions that we have had over the last few months. I also want to thank all of the members of our Consulting Network who have contributed to this book. A special thanks to Jean Hauser, Caroline Fischer, Michael McNally, Bill Mobley, Linda Reece, Meg Davis, Alejandro Rodriquez, Chris Cancialosi, and Brian Glaser.

Perhaps the most valued contributions came from those who helped us understand their organizations. They were open and insightful and shared a lot with us. Andreas Beerli and Patrick Mallieux of Swiss Re; Rolf Schlue of DeutscheTech; Dave Brandon, Patrick Doyle, and Patti Wilmot of Domino's; Tim Kuppler of GT Automotive; Matti Lehtonen of GE; and Roger Agnelli and Marco Dalpozza of Vale—they all helped us a lot! It is their achievements that make up the best lessons in this book.

Finally, my editor at Jossey-Bass, Kathe Sweeney, was a real pleasure to work with. She pushed and pulled and was a key part of the team all through the process. My thanks to her and all the staff at Jossey-Bass and Wiley who helped bring this project to completion.

In the end, of course, this book is dedicated to our families. They are the most important ones of all. Without their support, patience, and understanding, we never would have made it!

Lausanne, Switzerland   Daniel Denison
June 2012

The Authors

Daniel Denison is professor of management and organization at the International Institute for Management Development (IMD) in Lausanne, Switzerland, and is also chairman and founding partner of Denison Consulting, LLC, in Ann Arbor, Michigan. Dr. Denison received his bachelor's degree in psychology, sociology, and anthropology from Albion College and his Ph.D. in organizational psychology from the University of Michigan. He has written several books, including *Corporate Culture and Organizational Effectiveness*, published by Wiley in 1990. His writings have appeared in a number of leading journals including *Academy of Management Journal, Academy of Management Review, Administrative Science Quarterly, Organization Science, Organizational Dynamics, Journal of Organizational Behavior, Human Resource Management*, and *Policy Studies Review*. Professor Denison's research, teaching, and consulting focus on organizational culture and its impact on the performance and effectiveness of organizations. (Email: denison@imd.ch)

Robert Hooijberg has a Ph.D. from the University of Michigan and teaches at IMD in Lausanne. His areas of special interest are leadership and 360-degree feedback, negotiations, team building, and organizational culture. Before joining IMD in September 2000, Professor Hooijberg taught at Rutgers University in their MBA and Executive MBA programs in New Jersey, Singapore, and Beijing. In 1997, while at the Rutgers

Business School, he was named Professor of the Year by both the MBA students and the faculty.

Mr. Hooijberg's research has appeared in such journals as *Academy of Management Learning and Education Journal*, *Leadership Quarterly*, *Journal of Management*, *Human Relations*, *Organization Science*, *Human Resource Management*, *Hospital and Health Services Administration*, *Journal of Applied Social Psychology*, *Journal of Management Education*, *Administration & Society*, *International Journal of Organizational Analysis*, and *Journal of Organizational Behavior*. In 2007 he published an edited collection entitled *Being There Even When You Are Not: Leading Through Strategy, Structures, and Systems*.

He has provided programs for and consulted with organizations such as Vale, Wavin, WWL, Ernst & Young, DSM, Rabobank, Axel Springer, Credit Suisse, EMC, Novo Nordisk, Carlsberg, DNV, HSBC, Unilever, Bekaert, Roche Pharmaceuticals, Roche Vitamins, PSE&G, the U.S. Environmental Protection Agency, Merck, AT&T, Korea Telecom, Lucent, the Dutch Ministry of Social Affairs and Employment, and Horizon Blue Cross Blue Shield of New Jersey.

Nancy Lane (M.Sc., London School of Economics) is a researcher at IMD in Lausanne whose work focuses on coaching effectiveness and leadership. Before joining IMD she worked in the financial services industry. She earned her bachelor's in economics from the University of California at Berkeley.

Colleen Lief is a research associate working with IMD on corporate culture, leadership, and change management projects. She earned a master of philosophy degree in economics from the University of Glasgow, Scotland, and a bachelor of science degree in business administration from Duquesne University, Pittsburgh. Ms. Lief worked for over twenty years as a commercial banker at major financial institutions in the United States.

Index

Page references followed by *fig* indicate a figure; followed by *t* indicate a table.

A

Adaptability: Apple's case study on, 12–14; corporate culture's impact on, 2, 6, 7; creating change, customer focus, organizational learning dimensions of, 7, 8*fig*; Domino's Pizza (2001, 2003, 2004, 2006), 30*fig*–31, 32*fig*, 34*fig*, 36*fig*–37*fig*; GE Healthcare's CSW (Clinical Systems Wuxi) [2007], 119*fig*, 122*fig*–123*fig*; global purchasing department's strategic alignment of, 63*fig*; GT Automotive's HVAC North America, 95*fig*, 98*fig*, 102*fig*, 106*fig*; Polar Bank (2004), 75*fig*; Swiss Re Americas Division (2000 and 2002), 60*fig*; Vale (2006, 2008), 140*fig*, 146*fig*; Vale versus Inco (2006, 2008), 142*fig*, 147*fig*

Agnelli, Roger, 135–136, 137

Alstom (France), 113

AmBev (Brazil), 133

AMCI Holdings, 144, 146

Americas Division. *See* Swiss Re's Americas Division

Anheuser-Busch (USA), 133

Apple: adaptability of, 12–14; App Store innovation of, 13–14; mindset focusing on customer ecosystem, 14

Arcelor, 133

ArcelorMittal, 133

Artifacts: definition of, 3, 4*fig*; organizational cultural level of analysis, 153

B

Bad habits: rethinking and trying again in case of new, 158*fig*, 167–169; unlearning and leaving behind old, 158*fig*–161

Bad new habits: GE's approach to improving product quality, 168–169; GT Automotive's service learning methods in European transformation, 168; rethinking and trying again, 167–169; Vale's centralized approach to integrating the Inco acquisition, 167

Bad old habits: fiefdoms at Vale, 160–161; old HR process at Domino's, 159; sales process at DeutscheTech, 160; unlearning and leaving behind, 158*fig*–161

Bain Capital: Domino's Pizza purchased by, 27; reporting on Domino's investment by, 29; strategy based on people as competitive advantage, 22

Bartlett, Chris, 42–43

Beerli, Andreas, 57, 65–66

Beliefs: definition of, 3, 4*fig*; organizational cultural level of analysis, 153

"Belonging" standard, 47

Bharti Airtel, 133, 148

BlackBerry, 13

Board restructuring, 79–80

Boer Wars (South Africa), 156

Bombardier (Canada), 113

Boston Consulting Group (BCG), 133, 134, 148

Denison and Lief's role during, 96; exporting culture change examined through, 23, 92–93; HVAC Division transformation, 93–107t; HVAC North America's Culture Survey used during, 94, 95fig, 102fig, 106fig; improved HVAC culture change results, 107t; involvement meetings during, 94–96; lessons for leaders from, 107–111; North America/Europe culture change during, 100t–101t; rethinking service learning methods in European transformation, 168
Gunfire at Sea (Morrison), 155–156
Guo Song, 116

H

Habits: changing culture by changing, 158fig; difficulty of changing, 156–157, 166–167; evolution of naval artillery innovation story on, 155–156; as the "flywheel of society," 154; introduced as framework for leading culture change, 157–158fig; inventing and perfecting good new, 158fig, 164–167; learning to trade old ones for new, 154–157; preserving and strengthening good old, 158fig, 161–164; rethinking and retrying bad new, 158fig, 167–169; unlearning and discarding old bad, 158fig–161. See also Knowledge; Rituals; Routines
The Halo Effect (Rosenzweig), 5
Hansen, Katarina: creating one leadership development process, 80–81; creating one Polar Bank board, 79–80; creating one team, 80; Culture Survey response by, 77; decisions regarding misaligned managers, 85; developing one strategy at Polar Bank, 77–78; as Polar Bank's CEO, 73; tracking Polar Bank's transformation by, 74, 81, 83
Harrah's Entertainment, 45
Hindalco (India), 149–150
Holliday, Chad, 50
Hooijberg, Robert, 142
Hormosan Pharma (Germany), 133
HP-EDS merger: background information on, 71–72; integration challenges faced during, 72–73

HVAC North America. See GT Automotive case study

I

IBM, 133
IBM Consulting, 89
Iceberg image, 3, 4fig, 5
IKEA: flatpack element of IKEA system, 11–12; "The IKEA Way" strategy, 12; mission grows out of core beliefs and assumptions, 10–12
InBev, 133
Inco (Canada): cultural differences between Vale and, 141, 143–144; Culture Survey results on Vale versus Inco (2006), 142fig; Culture Survey results on Vale versus Inco (2008), 147fig; rethinking Vale's centralized approach to integrating, 167; Vale's acquisition of, 141
Indal (India), 149–150
Innovation: habits as framework for culture change and, 157–169; naval artillery, 155–156
Institute of Computing Technology (CAS), 150
Integration: communicating one message for, 78–79; creating one board for, 79–80; creating one corporate center for, 79; creating one leadership development process for, 80–81; creating one team for, 80; developing one strategy for, 77–78; Domino's Pizza (2001, 2003, 2004, 2006), 30fig–31, 32fig, 34fig, 36fig–37fig; GE Healthcare case study on challenge of culture, 122–124; of Inco and Vale's cultures, 141–147fig, 167; lessons for leaders on, 83–85; merger challenge of, 72–73, 86; Polar Bank case study on, 23, 73–85; tracking the transformation for, 81, 83. See also Corporate culture change; Corporate cultures; Mergers; Strategic alignment
Integration lessons: build cross-business capability, 85; create a common governance structure, 83–84; engage leaders in building common strategy, 84; make quick decisions about misaligned managers, 85